Praise for *The Manager's Communication Toolkit*

"Tina has written the 'how to' book on not only managing difficult personalities but also building productive relationships. Every manager—from the CEO down to the most junior person—should read this book and keep it close for reference. A must-read."

—**SID FUCHS**, defense industry CEO and author of *Get Off the Bench*

"Workforces are complex and diverse living organisms that are essential to an organization's success. Anyone—managers, senior staff, and new employees—who wants to understand and improve their interactions with colleagues and the workforce in general needs to first read this book and then adopt it as a reference guide on how to identify the different personalities that comprise their workforce, the types of communications strategies they could tailor to their particular situation, and the tools they could use to achieve successful outcomes. Tina Kuhn shows readers how to develop a vibrant and productive workforce."

—**LESLIE LEWIS, PHD**, consultant and recognized expert on strategic and business planning for the government and industry

"Whether you're a novice supervisor or a seasoned executive, this book is for you. The core of personal and professional success is effective communication. Tina's instruction in using the ten models of personality types gives realistic context to her book. You can easily translate her examples to your everyday work environment and may find yourself sorting your peers, managers, and employees into one of the ten personality types. Her practical leadership advice is a terrific annual checklist to remind us of how to be our best manager self."

—**JILL SINGER**, Vice President—National Security, AT&T

The MANAGER'S *Communication* TOOLKIT

TOOLS AND TECHNIQUES FOR
LEADING DIFFICULT PERSONALITIES

The MANAGER'S
Communication
TOOLKIT

TINA KUHN

GREENLEAF
BOOK GROUP PRESS

Published by Greenleaf Book Group Press

Austin, Texas
www.gbgpress.com

Distributed by Greenleaf Book Group

For ordering information or special discounts for bulk purchases, please contact Greenleaf Book Group at PO Box 91869, Austin, TX 78709, 512.891.6100.

Design and composition by Greenleaf Book Group
Cover design by Greenleaf Book Group and Chantel Stull
Cover image Sergey Korkin, 2018. Used under license from Shutterstock.com.

Publisher's Cataloging-in-Publication data is available.

Print ISBN: 978-1-62634-589-8

eBook ISBN: 978-1-62634-590-4

Part of the Tree Neutral® program, which offsets the number of trees consumed in the production and printing of this book by taking proactive steps, such as planting trees in direct proportion to the number of trees used: www.treeneutral.com

TreeNeutral®

Printed in the United States of America on acid-free paper

18 19 20 21 22 23   10 9 8 7 6 5 4 3 2 1

First Edition

*I dedicate this book to every project lead,
manager, and leader who is working to create good
communication and unity within their team.*

Table of Contents

Why Read This Book?

Do you have difficult people in your life? Do you sometimes feel frustrated by others' behavior or choices? Do you ever struggle when trying to communicate or work with a colleague, team member, boss, or customer? Do you have problems that remain unresolved despite your best efforts? Do you avoid dealing with issues because of fear of conflict? Do you want to become a better leader?

If you answered yes to any of these questions, then this book is for you.

Communication is the core of all management and leadership. Effective communication unites teams and provides a framework for a vision and goal to be met. Noted program manager authority Rita Mulcahy states, "Project managers spend 90 percent of their time on communication-related activities."[1] I would extrapolate from that and say that all good leaders spend 90 percent or more of their time communicating.

To be a good leader, you must be able to communicate effectively to all different types of people, using different styles and mediums. Keeping your organization or team focused on goals and avoiding the mire of drama and frustration depends on successfully dealing with even the most difficult people. This book teaches you how to present yourself, how to listen and respond to others, how to recognize stress in yourself and others, and how to resolve conflict. You will learn strategies for dealing with the ten most challenging personality types. These include the **Manipulator**, **Gossiper**, **Naysayer**, **Controller**, **Perfectionist**, **Yes-Man**, **Drama Queen**, **Recluse**, **Whiner**, and **Liar**. You will receive advice on how to adapt your communication to work with these difficult individuals and resolve conflict in a way that fosters greater teamwork and keeps everyone moving forward for the good of the organization.

As a senior executive with thirty-five years of expertise in organizational transformation, I have seen the results of good communication techniques and the consequences of poor ones. The ideas presented here come from years' worth of notes, gathered as I grew and learned how to be a better leader and communicator. I have worked in environments spanning the cybersecurity, defense, intelligence, government, and commercial industries. The businesses might have differed, but the communication issues I witnessed were remarkably similar from organization to organization. I have tackled dysfunctional teams and made them more unified, productive, and happy. It is an amazing feeling to see how some simple changes in communication make a huge difference in team unity, morale, productivity, teamwork, and happiness.

I am excited to share my knowledge of overcoming personality and communication issues to help you create a better working environment. The communication techniques described in this book draw on wide experience and interviews with leaders in numerous industries. From the information in this book, you will be able to understand and communicate with the diverse individuals in your organization, as well as identify their varying needs, their preferences, and the styles of communication that will be most effective for them.

THIS BOOK HAS ANSWERS.

By reading *The Manager's Communication Toolkit: Tools and Techniques for Leading Difficult Personalities*, you will acquire the insight, tools, and techniques to be a good communicator and leader. You will learn how to focus your conversations to make them more productive, meaningful, unifying, and comfortable. Your team and organization will progress quickly toward better conclusions. The communication techniques outlined in this book will help you become a self-aware, compassionate, and fair manager. By reading this book and applying its principles, you will also be able to identify what triggers you have and develop methods to maintain your personal top performance level at all times.

This book is divided into three parts. The first part of the book discusses how effective communication can unite teams and bring out the best in each person. It breaks down the different communication tools, which have advantages and disadvantages, depending on the situation and people involved. Effective communication takes into account the situation, relationship, and personality.

In the second part of the book, you will learn to recognize different difficult behavior types. Not only will I teach you to identify them, but I will also give you techniques to work with individuals who exhibit these behaviors. No matter what difficult personalities you may encounter in your day-to-day routine—your boss, your customers, your coworkers, or your team members—the tools in this book will help you communicate effectively, purposefully, and skillfully.

The third part of the book explores your own communication and management styles. Knowing how you react in situations will enable you to adapt both your communication and leadership abilities for maximum positive benefits. Using compassionate confrontation techniques provides a framework to more effectively tackle problems, remove roadblocks, and move ahead in an environment of respect and open communication. Finally, this book provides five traits of a great leader and steps you can take to become a highly effective leader.

WHO SHOULD READ THIS BOOK?

This book is for anyone who has to communicate with others at work. That includes bosses, coworkers, subordinates, and customers. It gives you a framework to have less conflict, better communication, and stronger leadership techniques. In fact, because communication is at the heart of all human interaction, this book will help anyone who seeks better communication skills as a means of improving daily life. The techniques introduced here can be applied to working with all people in every aspect of your everyday routine. It can and will positively influence all of your relationships: at work, at home, at school . . . wherever you go.

In preparing to write this book, I researched troubled projects, teams, and organizations. In all cases, communication was at the heart of the problem. Once the communication challenges were solved, other problems were quickly resolved. Given this understanding, it is clear that managers who expect to perform at the levels demanded by the current professional environment must be, above all, skilled and effective communicators. By reading and applying the ideas found in this book, you are taking the all-important first step toward making yourself the type of communicator your profession demands.

The Manager's Communication Toolkit shares the experiences of managers from multiple organizations with whom I worked over the years. Their stories are filled with dramatic, encouraging, and sometimes poignant lessons learned. Even though their experiences cross many different industries, the stories have a similar conclusion:

Effective communication is the core of successful management and leadership.

This book will save you, your team, your organization, and your business time and money. In today's extremely competitive environment, the bottom line cannot tolerate time wasted on internal squabbles or organizational disarray caused by disruptive and difficult behavior. Knowing how to motivate your team members by utilizing their strengths and personality types will help you and your team get activities completed on time, earn bonuses, and economize for your customers or your business.

Ultimately, everything in life is about communication and relationships. By reading this book, you will become aware of your own communication style and the communication style and preferences of others in order to adjust proactively before problem situations become insurmountable. This book provides the insight, tools, and techniques you need in order to become a confident leader capable of running a top-notch organization or project.

Personality Types and Communication Tools

Effective communication is about using the right tool and approach for the situation. In order to do that, you have to understand human relationships and the different communication preferences of the people involved—including yourself. In this first part, you will learn how different personality types—especially difficult ones—require different communication techniques. The more you know about each team member and how they like to communicate, the more effective and efficient you will become.

You will also develop a more in-depth understanding of the different communication tools available in a work environment. These include email, texting, face-to-face conversations, telephone conversations, meetings, presentations, and written reports. Each method available to you offers advantages and disadvantages, depending on the situation and people involved, and we will explore these.

Effective communication not only looks at the personalities and tools involved but also the social relationship and situation. Situations can be formal or informal; the relationship can vary from a new boss to a team member to long-term friendly coworkers and anything in between.

Finally, this part discusses why it is important to know the personality types of each person. Each individual has certain attributes that make particular formats and styles of communication more or less effective when communicating to that individual. It is up to the manager to know what to use, with whom, and when.

This section gives you a framework to motivate your team members. By utilizing their strengths, you can develop a high-functioning team so your organization will meet its goals.

Chapter 1

Understanding Different Personality Types

Most organizations are only as successful as their leadership. As a leader, you have multiple lines of responsibility to your subordinates, coworkers, supervisors, and clients. Balancing everything can be a delicate, demanding, and exhausting task. Success depends on knowing as much as you can about the most important assets your organization has: the people—including yourself—on whom you depend to make everything happen. In this chapter, we'll take a look at the various types of people you might expect to interact with, trying to learn the most effective ways of ensuring good communication with each type.

Being an effective leader and communicator depends on understanding yourself and others. For managers to communicate effectively, they should understand what motivates and drives each person they encounter, which can provide a framework for rapid assessment of strategies to bring about a successful outcome. It provides a method to observe and understand your own behavior and that of others and to analyze conflicts and miscommunications, enabling you to resolve them in a positive manner.

Many different models exist to describe the different dimensions of individual personality. In my experience, the most useful practice focuses on diagnosing and neutralizing negative behavior patterns. When people feel stressed, they may resort to undesirable behaviors as defense mechanisms. The negative behaviors can manifest in any of the following ways: manipulation, gossip, naysaying, controlling, perfectionism, people pleasing, drama, reclusiveness, whining, and lying. The more information you have about a colleague or subordinate's personality and communication preferences, the greater the likelihood you'll be able to defuse potential stress and generate positive interactions. As a manager, recognizing the uniqueness of those with whom you work is crucial for assessing, connecting, motivating, and resolving conflict.

When a leader takes the time to listen to and observe those around them, they become more adept at identifying individual motivations. Whether you are meeting someone for the first time or talking to someone you have known for twenty years, shifting your behavior and tailoring the interaction to their personality will lead to more effective communication and better relationships.

EFFECTIVE COMMUNICATION WITH DIFFERENT PERSONALITIES

Different personality types require different techniques for the most effective communication. How do you communicate in your organization or team? Do you know how much contact the people you communicate with prefer or need? Does your boss need to hear from you frequently to feel comfortable that your tasks are going as planned? Does your customer prefer email, phone calls, or face-to-face meetings? These questions are worth considering, because the more you know about how people like to communicate, the better rapport and relationships you will be able to establish—and the more efficient your organization, tasks, or project will be. An effective manager collaborates and builds relationships at all levels of the workplace community.

Poor communication can compromise your reputation and effectiveness. Any person (team member, boss, coworker, customer, end user, member of another department, someone in the broader community) can either derail or promote an activity, project, or task. To leverage the whole community, you must build relationships with all stakeholders. Good communication skills help build good relationships.

Some relationships will be easy: communication will flow back and forth smoothly. With others, the road to effective communication is bumpy and not much fun. In these cases, already-difficult relationships can be compounded to unmanageable levels of stress during a crisis. To navigate those situations, leaders must be able to manage themselves as well as their teams. Moving forward depends on the manager's ability to think clearly and rationally.

To be a good manager, you must be able to communicate effectively to all different types of people in a variety of styles and mediums. The good news is that these techniques work no matter who you are dealing with. The subsequent chapters will teach you how to adapt your communication in order to work with various types of individuals: how to present yourself, how to listen and respond to others, how to recognize stressed people, and how to effectively resolve conflict.

To get started, of course, you need to understand yourself. This includes not only your communication preferences but also the tools that are available to you, which we will explore in the next chapter.

Chapter 2

Your Communication ToolKit

Just as different people have differing communication styles and needs, you have at your disposal tools with differing capabilities. Depending on the situation and the person with whom you are communicating, some will be more suitable than others. This chapter will help you establish ground rules for choosing the best tool for a given scenario and communication partner.

We have a variety of communications media available: face-to-face and telephone conversations, email, texting, group meetings, presentations, and written reports. Each can be effective if it is used in the right context, but each can be disastrous if used in the wrong way. People with different personality types are not all equally comfortable with any single given tool, and the higher the stakes, the more critical it is for you to choose the most appropriate method for the other person in the situation. After all, when you are going into a potentially stressful interaction, it does you little good to have other people on edge any more than necessary. It is up to you as the manager to ensure that you and your team utilize the correct communication tool for each situation.

There are four basic groups of communication tools widely used in the workplace:

1. **Face-to-face (including video teleconferencing) and telephone communication** are individual meetings with you and one other person. Face-to-face meetings are the most effective type of communication technique for building rapport, collaboration, or confrontation.

2. **Email and texting** are written, nearly instantaneous messages extensively used in the workforce. Email and texting are ubiquitous but may help or harm, depending on the message and situation.

3. **Group meetings and presentations** involve multiple people meeting together. Presentations are group meetings with prepared information to describe and/or review. Both are great for keeping everyone on the same page but challenging to keep on track.

4. **Written reports** are formal written documents. Reports are effective for documenting information multiple people need to agree upon or approve.

Let's talk about basic communication tools and the benefits and pitfalls of each.

FACE-TO-FACE AND TELEPHONE COMMUNICATION

When it comes to communication intended to foster collaboration, confrontation, or to conduct any other type of sensitive conversation that could cause an emotional reaction, face-to-face (including video teleconferences) and telephone communication work better than email and texting. In face-to-face discussions you have access to all the body's signals:

words, body language, gestures, paralinguistic interaction (voice, volume inflection, and pitch), facial expressions, and appearance. An estimated 93 percent of human communication is nonverbal and paralinguistic; these cues provide valuable information to your communication partner, determining in many cases how your message is received. Further, another person's nonverbal, paralinguistic, and body-language feedback can help you perceive and adjust what you say and how you are saying it to be most effective. In face-to-face and telephone conversations, active listening is an extremely important component. Often when people talk to each other, they do not listen attentively. They are distracted, half listening, or busy formulating a response to what is being said. Especially in situations involving frequent communication partners, people assume they have heard what the other person is saying many times before, so rather than paying attention, they focus on how they can respond to prove their point or win the argument.

Active listening has several benefits. First, it forces people to listen attentively to others in order to be able to accurately reflect back what has been said. Second, it avoids misunderstandings, because listeners have to confirm that they do really understand what another person has said. Third, it tends to open people up, to get them to say more. In active listening, the listener does not have to agree with the speaker but still works hard to understand and repeat what the speaker said. If the listener has not properly understood, the speaker can further explain. Active listening is especially useful

> "Active listening is an important way to bring about changes in people. Despite the popular notion that listening is a passive approach, clinical and research evidence clearly shows that sensitive listening is a most effective agent for individual personality change and group development. Listening brings about changes in peoples' attitudes toward themselves and others; it also brings about changes in their basic values and personal philosophy. People who have been listened to in this new and special way become more emotionally mature, more open to their experiences, less defensive, more democratic, and less authoritarian."[1]

during confrontation. (There is more information on confrontation techniques in chapter 15.)

FACE-TO-FACE COMMUNICATION

In face-to-face conversations (including video conferences), your body gestures and posture (i.e., body language) can help you communicate your message. Make sure your body language gives the same message as your words. Your body position and gestures give other people cues about your thoughts and emotions. Body language varies from culture to culture, and what is polite in one culture may be offensive in another. For example, in Russia, to smile a lot conveys that you are not trustworthy; in the United States, smiling is the way to connect with people. In Japan, eye contact is considered rude; in the United States, if you don't look people in the eye, you are not considered sincere. If you will be directly communicating with people from another culture, you should learn their norms.

In any situation involving face-to-face communication, it is important to stay engaged in the current conversation. So many times, cell phones and other interruptions distract you and have the effect of making the person you are talking to feel unimportant. In some cases, it may be appropriate or necessary to accept a call, but please apologize and explain why the interruption is necessary. In fact, if you anticipate an urgent or important call, it is a good idea to alert your communication partner at the start of a conversation.

Let's look at two face-to-face scenarios. In the first scenario, interruptions damage an important personal connection. In the second scenario, an employee does not take the time to understand his communication partner's preferences.

Arthur was the manager of a large telecommunication project. One day he walked around introducing the new design engineer, Tom, to team members. Arthur introduced Tom to Oren, a senior technician. While Oren was explaining his job, Stacey, the business manager, approached and said, "Arthur, I need to talk to you about the overrun of the installation costs." Oren heard the question and lost his train of thought; he didn't know the project had overrun the cost and wanted to hear Arthur's answer. Tom noticed that Oren kept looking over at Arthur and Stacey. Feeling slightly awkward, Tom said, "Well, it was nice to meet you, Oren." Arthur finally told Stacey and Oren that they would have to talk about it later. He then introduced Tom to Stacey, who said, "Welcome aboard," but quickly walked away. Arthur felt his cell phone buzz and pulled it out to check his email. Tom was left standing in the hall while Arthur read.

The interchange left Tom feeling he was unimportant to the organization. Arthur clearly didn't believe introducing him was a priority.

Let's look at a way both Arthur and Stacey could have handled this better.

Arthur was the manager of a large telecommunication project. He had a new design engineer, Tom. On Tom's first day, Arthur walked him around to introduce him to the team. He introduced Tom to Oren, a senior technician, who proceeded to tell Tom his role on the project.

Stacey, the business manager, saw Tom engaged with Oren and approached Arthur, stating, "I need to talk to you urgently after you finish introducing the new employee around." Arthur said, "I will come to your office immediately after I am finished." She then approached Tom to say, "Welcome aboard, we are glad to have you here. I'm the business manager, and I will set up a meeting tomorrow so we can talk in depth about the project." She walked back to her office to wait for Arthur.

Arthur felt his cell phone buzz but ignored it while he introduced Tom to the rest of the team.

Stacey waited until Tom was engaged with Oren before she pulled Arthur aside. She didn't talk about her urgent issue in the hallway but simply requested Arthur come and see her when he was done walking Tom around. She then introduced herself to let Tom know he was important to her. In refraining from using his smart phone, Arthur also let Tom know he was important.

Joe and his new boss, Larry, had their first monthly face-to-face meeting to touch base and review the status of multiple teams Joe managed. Joe walked in with a few ideas for conversation topics but had nothing written down. Joe's previous boss had been a friend for thirty years, and their relationship at work was very informal. Larry, on the other hand, had different expectations. He anticipated a more formal relationship that included written status reports and detailed metrics for each team. Joe offered verbal updates but could not answer detailed cost and schedule questions. Larry, frustrated, began checking email on his phone while Joe talked. Both men walked out of the meeting feeling frustrated.

In this scenario, both made erroneous assumptions on the other's communication preferences. Larry should have communicated to Joe his expectations for the meeting. For his part, Joe failed to ask Larry what he wanted to see and how it should be presented. Once he realized the disconnect between his expectations and Joe's preparation, Larry, as the supervisor, should have simply stopped the meeting, explained to Joe what he expected, and rescheduled. Instead, he let the meeting continue, only to subsequently dismiss Joe by paying more attention to his phone. Joe, noticing Larry's dissatisfaction, could have chosen to apologize, find out what he wanted, and set up a briefing time with the material and formats Larry preferred.

Let's look at the scenario again when Larry and Joe communicated appropriately and set expectations ahead of the meeting.

Larry, new to the organization, set up a monthly, reoccurring status meeting with Joe, a manager under him. Larry sent an agenda of the topics he expected to cover, describing which items should be provided in written format and which could be verbal.

When Joe saw the meeting notice, he groaned. This was far more detailed than meetings with his previous boss. Still, Joe worked hard in the next few days to gather and write up all the information Larry requested. He pulled together a detailed status of the cost, schedule, risk, and customer relations for each project. As a result, he did see some issues he had not noticed before because he ran the projects so informally. Joe had a busy few days working the issues before the monthly status meeting.

During the meeting, Joe was able to discuss each project in detail, and provided Larry status documents for later review. Larry felt he had an excellent manager who was able to juggle multiple projects successfully, and felt proud of the team's accomplishments.

Larry communicated to Joe what he expected. Joe listened to Larry and provided the requested information. Joe also saw the value of gathering and analyzing the information Larry wanted to see. Both Larry and Joe were happy with their first status meeting, and the relationship got off to a good start.

Potential Q's

Face-to-Face Conversation Do's

✓ If you have not met before, introduce yourself and ask the other person's name.

✓ Use the person's name to show you are really paying attention and connecting.

✓ Leave conversations on a high note; people remember best what is said last.

✓ Articulate the purpose of the meeting. Prepare for your conversation.

✓ Be polite and respectful. Say "please" and "thank you."

✓ Be mindful of people's time and keep the conversation brief.

Face-to-Face Conversations Don'ts

✗ Don't interrupt when someone else is talking.

✗ Don't fidget, look around, or get up from your chair when another person is talking to you.

✗ Don't make disparaging remarks about others, whether they are present or absent.

✗ Pick your battles. Don't argue about things that are not important.

✗ Don't use accusatory statements; they will put the other person immediately on the defensive.

✗ Don't change the focus of the conversation until you are sure all parties are ready to move on to a different topic.

TELEPHONE COMMUNICATION

Telephone conversations require some discipline to be effective. There are no body language or facial expressions to help convey the message, so the words, tone, and inflection alone must do the job. The natural cadence between people when they talk is also disrupted due to the lack of visual clues as to when the other person is finished speaking. Let's look at a telephone scenario. The following scenario shows a person unprepared for the phone conversation.

Edna: Hello.

Jacob: Is Edna there?

Edna: Speaking.

Jacob: I am new to the project and would like to get updated.

Edna: Who I am speaking to?

Jacob: This is Jacob Allen.

Edna: How are you affiliated with the project?

Jacob: I am taking over the government quality auditor position that Jennifer Stipes used to do.

Edna: So you are going to be the contact person now? Do you want a copy of the most recent status reports?

Jacob: Yes, and can I get on the email list for future reports?

Edna: Yes, let me get your contact information and I will send the report.

In this scenario, the first impression given by the customer is confusion; who Jacob is and the reason for his phone call are not clear. The receiver has to take the lead in the conversation.

The following scenario describes a more polished and professional way to handle the discussion.

Edna: Edna Lange, DNA Analysis Manager.

Jacob: Is Edna Lange available?

Edna: Speaking.

Jacob: Hi, this is Jacob Allen. I am replacing Jennifer Stipes as the government quality auditor. Is this a good time to speak with you for a couple of minutes?

Edna: Yes, thank you, now would be fine.

Jacob: I would like to receive the most recent status and also get on the email list to receive future communications.

Edna: Sure, no problem. Welcome aboard! Would you like to set up a time to meet face-to-face and have a walkthrough of the lab area?

Jacob: Yes, I would love to come out to see the facility, thank you very much. I am free all day tomorrow if that is not too soon.

Edna: Tomorrow is great. How about 9:00 a.m.?

Jacob: I look forward to working with you. I will send you my contact information so you have it for your records.

Edna: Thank you. I will see you tomorrow at 9.

This conversation works because the caller identifies who he is and gets straight to the point. The communication is clear, direct, and doesn't take up any unnecessary time. Both speakers are professional and helpful, and the conversation ends on a positive note.

Telephone etiquette is a part of the general impression you give people. Following are some do's and don'ts in telephone conversations.

Phone Conversation Do's

✓ Introduce yourself immediately so the caller doesn't have to guess who is on the line.

✓ Leave conversations on a high note. People remember best what is said last.

✓ Have a purpose to your phone conversation. Prepare for your call and articulate the purpose of your telephone call early in the conversation.

✓ Be polite and respectful. Say "please" and "thank you." Your listener cannot see your body language, so you must overcompensate by being very polite.

✓ Listen to what the other person is saying.

✓ Be very clear in what you say; don't assume the listener knows what you want.

✓ Keep conversations short.

✓ If the phone conversation is not planned and may be lengthy, ask if this is a good time to talk; your listener will appreciate your respect for his time.

✓ Be direct and get to the point. Be very mindful of the person's time.

Phone Conversations Don'ts

✗ Don't interrupt when someone else is talking.

✗ Don't use swear words. It is not only offensive to some people, it will make you appear less professional.

✗ Don't use accusatory statements. It will put the other person immediately on the defensive.

✗ Don't send emails or text messages while on the phone. You will not only miss what the person is saying, but they may hear the keystrokes and realize you are not paying attention to the conversation.

EMAIL AND TEXTING

Email and texting have become ubiquitous in our culture and are used for all types of communication. Because they are worldwide, are nearly instantaneous, and can be used to communicate with a number of people at the same time, email and texting can be powerful tools if used with discernment. While both are great for quick exchanges of information and data, they fall short of promoting or encouraging collaboration. Furthermore, email and texting should never be used for confrontation. Why? As respected human communications expert Albert Mehrabian proved, communication between humans is approximately 55 percent body language, 38 percent tone of voice, and 7 percent what you say.[2] With email and text, you remove the first 93 percent.

Emails and texts are very easy to write and send but also incredibly easy to misinterpret, simply because the personal element is almost completely missing. Much of what we feel and think comes out in our nonverbal communication. Emails and texting cannot provide nonverbal cues, so it is very easy to convey the wrong message and just as easy to receive and interpret an email or text incorrectly. While some may attempt to use "emojis" or texting codes such as "lol" ("laughing out loud") to convey emotional context, these shortcuts generally lack the professional tone that you will want to maintain as a manager. For all these reasons, if you need to have communication with someone that involves potentially emotional content or that must function to build rapport, email and texting are almost never the correct choices.

There are, however, instances when these rapid methods of communication can be extremely useful, so let's take a closer look at their principal strengths.

Email

Most managers receive a huge volume of email. To be most effective, emails need to have a clear purpose. If extended dialogue is required, communication should take place in a phone conversation, video teleconferencing, or meeting. However, email works well to disseminate information to a large number of people. It is asynchronous (the sender and receiver do not have to communicate at the same time), which works wonderfully for communicating to teams distributed across time

zones (or even on different continents), for information and data sharing, and for communication of noncritical or noncontroversial data.

The following scenario illustrates an overly detailed, complex email.
The customer, reading on her phone, saw only the first three lines and
missed the most important part. This led her to misinterpret what she
read and then to call the president of the company and complain about
the quality of the project team.

To: Customer

From: Project Team Lead

Subject: Status

For the application, the problem remaining is that a file and a database
field cannot be deleted from the record. We have not yet confirmed that
Batch is working—that is what we plan to do next. However, files can be
successfully deleted from other records. We have verified that the general
searches as well as the Admin functions are working.

If users try to log in now, they will be able to do all the functionality
above, as the application is currently running.

We would like to update the "Message of the Day" to indicate that
users should refrain from deleting files until further notice.

Please let me know if we should proceed with the above "Message
of the Day" change and continue to allow the application to run for
now with this known issue. Otherwise, we would need to shut down the
application.

As I mentioned, we will perform testing of Batch now (queries only)
and let you know the status.

Assuming that is successful, this would allow query-only Batch files
to be processed.

> We will also continue to work the delete issue mentioned above. However, at this time, we do not have an estimate for when this will be resolved. We are continuing to work the issue and report status.

The email did not get to the point fast enough and was full of technical jargon. It is very common for readers to just glance at the first part of an email before responding. In this case, she never read the part stating that the problem was solved.

But the following scenario suggests an example of a much better way to deliver the required information.

> To: Customer
> From: Project Team Lead
> Subject: Need permission to update Message of the Day
>
> The software application is up and running. We have resolved all but one of the issues: deletion of a file.
>
> We would like permission to update the "Message of the Day" to indicate that users should refrain from deleting files until further notice.
>
> We have our experts working on the delete issue and feel confident the final issue will be resolved in a timely manner.
>
> We will provide status later in the day. Please let us know if you would like more details on our approach.

This email is very clear on the question being asked and the response required. It omits unnecessary detail. The recipient can read it easily and send back a quick response.

Another facet of providing only the necessary detail: while

sometimes you actually need to forward an entire email chain (the exchanges between recipients and senders, appearing one above the other in reverse chronological order), there are other times when you should "snip the tails"—delete all but the message immediately preceding your response. If you do not, what started as a short exchange may grow into a multipage document by the time it has been passed around among a number of participants. For this reason, many discussion lists require the tails to be snipped.

Finally, make sure you are sending email only to those for whom it provides necessary information. This may involve deciding carefully who should be copied ("cc'ed" for their information only) on the message and who should be addressed directly (and perhaps expected to respond). Some offices have strict protocols for the use of the "cc" function; if yours is one of these, know the procedure and follow it.

Let's look at another example. The following scenario shows an email where multiple topics make it hard for the reader to keep track of all the requests enclosed.

To: Frank

From: Melinda

Subject: Issues

Frank,

I have several topics I need to discuss with you. The first one is that we need additional space for Project A. We are adding three new people to the project and do not have any additional cubes. It looks like project B is winding down, so we could take over some of their space. As an alternative, we could also move the entire project to our other building, so we have space to expand in the future.

I have heard from some of our technical team that the customer is talking about issuing a "Request for Proposal" for new work. I believe we are in a good position to bid on this job. I have a few ideas on how to position ourselves to be the best-qualified candidate, including developing a paper on our solution to give to the customer before they officially send out the request for proposal.

I also need permission to hire an administrative assistant. We are in desperate need of someone to take care of our administration tasks, and our team leads are all doing administration duties. I have talked to the customer and they are in favor of hiring an admin to free up more of the team leads' time.

Thank you very much,

Melinda

The preceding email has multiple subjects: starting a brainstorming discussion about a proposal; requesting permission to make a hire; and starting a discussion about options for facilities. All three of these subjects need to be handled in separate communications.

The following scenario is the better way to handle the communication.

To: Frank

From: Melinda

Subject: Additional Space Needed for Project A

Frank, we are running out of space on Project A. I see two options:

1. Take over adjacent space from Project B. The project is winding down and they have empty space.

2. Move to the other building, where there is lots of space to expand in the future.

Please let me know your preference.

Thanks,

Melinda

....

To: Frank

From: Melinda

Subject: Approval for hiring admin

Frank,

I would like permission to hire an administrative assistant for Project A. The customer has approved and we have funding.

Thank you very much,

Melinda

....

To: Frank, Project A Team Leads

From: Melinda

Meeting Notice: Oct 4

2:00 – 3:00

Subject: Opportunity for Growth on Project A

Please attend the meeting to discuss the opportunities for growth on Project A.

Each email in this scenario has a single subject and a clear definition of the response required. Also, note that a group meeting notice is sent to discuss the growth opportunity for Project A; a group meeting is a much better way to brainstorm.

Let's look at some email do's and don'ts.

Email Do's

✓ Limit to one subject per email and list it clearly in the subject line.

✓ Give the most important information in the first sentence. Get to the point right away.

✓ Specify who should respond to your email.

✓ Be clear on when you need a response. The due date can also be included in the subject.

✓ Provide a summary when you are forwarding a chain of emails.

✓ Use the "cc:" field only when necessary.

✓ Be polite. Terseness can be misinterpreted.

✓ Review all the "to:" and "cc:" lines before sending. This ensures the email gets to the correct people, and only to them.

✓ Always reread and then spell-check your emails before sending.

✓ Use normal capitalization and punctuation. Some people view emails with all lower case, misspellings, and texting shortcuts as unprofessional.

✓ Be sparing with large attachments. Many servers have email size limitations.

✓ As organization-recorded documents, all emails are organizational property. They can be used as legal documents.

✓ Avoid putting anything in an email that you wouldn't want to see on the front page of a newspaper or in court.

> ## Email Don'ts
>
> ✗ Don't escalate a conflict. Avoid email flaming (hostile and insulting emails); instead, request a face-to-face meeting or pick up the phone.
>
> ✗ Don't make assumptions if the email doesn't make any sense or something is unclear. Ask for explanation.
>
> ✗ Don't address more people in your email than necessary (don't overuse the "cc" field).
>
> ✗ Don't send or forward emails containing defamatory, offensive, racist, or obscene remarks.
>
> ✗ Don't overuse "Reply to All." Use only when absolutely necessary, and never use for disparaging information.
>
> ✗ Don't use all capitals in emails; this usually comes across as shouting. If you are angry, take some time to think about the situation and then talk to the person face-to-face.
>
> ✗ Never send an email with disparaging information about any person; chances are it will get back to them (and see last item on list of "do's," above).

Texting

Texting is a focused, one-on-one electronic communication technique that's somewhat like talking on the phone. Text messages are typically shorter and quicker than emails, and some shortcuts in typing are acceptable. It is an excellent technique for yes or no answers or quick information sharing.

Texting is also more casual than email and is great for communicating with people you already know. However, texting should be limited in a work environment. Text messages cannot be easily stored, forwarded, or archived; attachments usually cannot be added; and formatting is limited.

The following scenario shows example messages overusing text acronyms, shortcuts, and emoticons.

S – we r hving a f2f rlco in 10. can u b there? jon made me lol at the mtg this mrning. I almost pmp.

ttfn

F – thnx for the heads up i can go. imho bob is boring is he spking today? I hope not

c u soon

S – re the action at mtg do u hv the l8est financial #s?

F – 1 sec

F – sent via email

As with email, it is not appropriate to make negative remarks about another person. Frank should have refrained from stating he thought Bob was boring. Writing out sentences is more professional and does not take significantly more time. In addition, full sentences will help avoid confusion for readers who may not know texting shortcuts. For example: **pmp** is the common acronym for the Program Manager Institute's "Program Manager Professional" certification. In texting, however, "pmp" also means "peed my pants"—not a professional comment, by most standards. Remember, text messages often can be accessed for legal action.

The following scenario illustrates a much more polished and professional exchange of information. This is a better, more professional way to have handled the texting.

Sharron – We are having a meeting in 10 minutes. Can you attend? Jon made me laugh at the meeting this morning. He is so funny.

Frank – Thanks for the meeting notice. I can attend. Yes, Jon is funny.

Sharron – In regards to the action I received in the meeting today, do you have the latest financial spreadsheet? I need it to finish my action.

Frank – I sent the financial spreadsheet file to you via email.

Let's look at the do's and don'ts for texting in the workplace:

Texting Do's

✓ Be polite. Terseness can be misinterpreted.

✓ Use texting for short communications and quick answers.

✓ Use normal capitalization and punctuation. Texting with all lower case, misspellings, and texting shortcuts can be interpreted as unprofessional.

✓ Treat all workplace text messages as though they are being sent to your boss or the local newspaper. Make sure you would feel comfortable with all your text messages being publicized.

Texting Don'ts

✗ Don't text during meetings or while talking to someone.

✗ Don't use texting for confrontation.

✗ Don't overuse text acronyms, shortcuts, or emoticons. Not everyone in the workplace is familiar with texting shortcuts.

✗ Don't send text messages containing defamatory, offensive, racist, or obscene remarks.

✗ Don't hide behind texting; it is not a suitable substitute for face-to-face conversations.

✗ Don't use all capitals in texting; this is assumed to be shouting. If you are angry, talk to the person face-to-face.

✗ Never send a text message with disparaging information about any person. Chances are it will get back to them (and see last item in list of texting do's, above).

MEETINGS AND PRESENTATIONS

Meetings and presentations have an important place in most offices and enterprises, as they streamline group communication and information sharing. Both may occur in a face-to-face setting, or via video and teleconferencing. However, they can be difficult to run effectively, because people bring in personal agendas to the event. It is paramount to have a clear agenda and to communicate the desired outcome at the start of a meeting or presentation.

Group meetings are an effective and necessary tool for managers. Meetings occur for many reasons, including sharing status and necessary information, brainstorming, or managing change. However, meetings need to be managed effectively, including the use of an agenda, advanced preparation, exercising control over the time spent on each topic, and taking written minutes to ensure all actions and decisions are documented.

Sometimes meetings are not effective because one person dominates and does not allow others to speak. The meeting leader must learn how to manage such disruptive individuals. Chapters 4–13 describe techniques to manage and lead different disruptive personality types. Group meetings should never be used for personal confrontation; this should be done one-on-one.

Teleconferencing and videoconferencing now allow remote attendance at many meetings. This poses additional challenges to the person managing the meeting. It is even more important to be clear about the agenda, the expected meeting outcome, and the time allotted for each topic. In teleconferences, if meeting attendees become disinterested, they may put the meeting on mute and do email, hold other conversations, and even walk away from the phone—hardly an efficient way to accomplish the goals of the meeting.

Following is an example of a project kickoff meeting with both in-person and teleconference attendees. In the first scenario, the project manager was not prepared for the meeting. The second scenario describes a better way to handle the meeting.

Sunil, a project manager, sauntered into his project kickoff meeting a minute or two late. His boss, Benjamin, had called the meeting to make sure all the departments were on the same page. There had been some confusion within the finance and contract departments at the start of the previous project Sunil managed, and Benjamin wanted this one to go more smoothly. He had given Sunil an agenda with the topics he wanted covered. Sunil didn't understand why his boss was making the kickoff a big deal. His previous projects had all worked out fine without one. He reluctantly gathered information but didn't spend much time or effort preparing. By the time Sunil arrived, the contracts and finance leads had been dialed in for five minutes. Sunil opened up his laptop and fumbled with his computer. Everyone could hear the sound of someone typing away on the teleconference line as Sunil got set up. At last, he started the meeting with some project basics and called for questions. Various participants started peppering him about the terms of the contracts, payment structure, contractual deliverables, invoicing, and staffing needs. Sunil did not know most of the answers, stumbled for a few minutes, and finally promised to get back to them soon. Meanwhile, typing could still be heard in the background.

At last, Benjamin stopped the meeting and said, "Sunil, we will reschedule this meeting for tomorrow after you gather all the information required."

Sunil had an agenda given to him by his boss, Benjamin, but he did not prepare adequately and did not have the necessary information to run the meeting effectively or efficiently. The people on the phone got distracted during the meeting because Sunil was so unprepared.

The next scenario describes how Sunil could have managed the meeting in a better way.

Sunil, a project manager, received a request from his boss, Benjamin, for a kickoff meeting on his new project. Benjamin gave Sunil an agenda with the topics he wanted covered. Sunil had never given a formal kickoff meeting before, so he had to work hard and pull all the required information together.

Sunil got to the conference room ten minutes early so he could make sure his briefing correctly displayed on the conference room screen. He also emailed the material to the remote attendees and dialed the teleconference number to ensure it was working.

Sunil went through the required information quickly. Thanks to his advance prep work, he answered all questions from the attendees. He left the meeting with a few action items, which he followed up within the day.

The whole team was on the same page and felt good about the project.

Sunil prepared the required material for the meeting, made sure the remote attendees had the material, and followed through on the actions.

Presentations are formal meetings that include prepared material; they usually take additional time and effort so material can be revised and polished until the data and intent are clear. A presentation is effective when communicating detailed information with the intent of producing a decision (e.g., a design presentation to a customer with the expectation that the customer will decide whether to proceed with the project). It is always a good idea to have a dry run of the presentation to ensure both presenter and material are clear, accurate, and make efficient use of the allotted time.

In the two scenarios that follow, we will explore successful and unsuccessful presentation techniques.

> The customer, users, and senior managers gathered in a large conference room to hear the presentation of the new system design. The team had worked days and nights on the project; the presenters performed two dry runs of the material to ensure the presentation was crisp and clear. Before the team started on their presentation, the company senior manager, Sam, stood up to say a few words. He started welcoming everyone, and then his cell phone rang. He answered the call and, standing in the front of the room, conversed with his administrative assistant about an office issue. Meeting attendees shifted restlessly and broke into side conversations. After a few minutes, Sam hung up and continued with his opening remarks. The meeting continued, but the energy in the room was flat, and the customer was distracted from the original purpose.

The senior manager, by his actions, set the wrong tone and told the customer she was less important than a phone call from his administrative assistant.

Let's look at a way this could have been handled with a different outcome.

> The customer, users, and senior managers gathered in a large conference room to hear the presentation of the new system design. The team had worked days and nights on the project; the presenters performed two dry runs of the material to ensure the presentation was crisp and clear. Before

the team started on their presentation, the company senior manager, Sam, stood up to say a few words. He started welcoming everyone, and his cell phone rang. He apologized, pulled his phone out, and put it on mute. Sam then finished his welcome and introduced the chief engineer who was conducting the meeting.

Sam did not let his cell phone take precedence over welcoming important customers and kicking off the system design review.

In this second scenario, the chief engineer, Jay, lost control of the meeting, throwing it into chaos.

On a very large project critical to the company's future, the team worked with the customer's engineers to create a design that met requirements. At the next meeting, they had two days' worth of material to present. After an introduction, the chief engineer, Jay, began describing top-level designs of the system. One audience member, representing the users of the system, repeatedly broke in to ask detailed questions and suggest that the design needed to be completely reworked. The lead customer engineer started arguing with him. Jay, not knowing what to do, stood to the side and let them argue. The discussion became extremely emotional and resulted in the lead user engineer throwing down his pen and storming out of the room.

Instead of taking charge of the meeting, Jay stepped aside and let an argument go unchecked. The atmosphere became emotional and destructive. Let's look at a better way for Jay to handle this difficult situation.

On a very large project critical to the company's future, the team worked with the customer's engineers to create a design that met requirements. At the next meeting, they had two days' worth of material to present. After an introduction, the chief engineer, Jay, began describing top-level designs of the system. One audience member, representing the users of the system, repeatedly broke in to ask detailed questions and suggest that the design needed to be completely reworked. The lead customer engineer started arguing with him.

Jay, recognizing the damage this type of argument could do to the meeting and the project as a whole, called a break. As everyone stood, Jay pulled aside the engineer representing the users aside. He said, "I hear your concerns. Let's meet tomorrow to address these issues." The engineer agreed.

When the meeting started up again, Jay told the audience about the planned meeting, promising to get an understanding of the concerns and work with the customer to incorporate the changes into the design.

Whenever the engineer representing the user started becoming agitated, Jay immediately put it on the list of issues to address the next day.

In this scenario, Jay immediately announced a break to give the two engineers time to calm down and have their needs addressed in private. He also asked the user engineer for specific items he felt would not work on the design, writing them down as action items for later, and requested the meeting continue.

Let's look at some group meeting, video teleconference meeting, and teleconference meeting do's and don'ts:

Meeting Do's

✓ Have a timed agenda and a clear purpose for the meeting.

✓ Start and end the meeting on time.

✓ Respect the people at the meeting by being polite; honor their need to participate in the conversations.

✓ Articulate the purpose and the desired outcome of the meeting.

✓ Close the meeting formally, thanking attendees for their time.

✓ Document all decisions and actions taken in the meeting.

✓ Turn your cell phone off (or explain at the beginning you are waiting for a call and may need to step out).

✓ Come prepared to the meeting and ask only relevant questions.

✓ Use active listening skills.

✓ Perform introductions if there are people in the meeting who may not know each other.

✓ Encourage the perspective of the entire group. Don't let the loudest or most talkative person run the show or determine the outcome.

Meeting Don'ts

✗ Don't interrupt when someone else is talking. Be polite and pay attention to each speaker.

✗ In a face-to-face meeting, don't fidget, look around, or get up from your chair when another person is talking to you.

✗ In a teleconference meeting, say your name before you speak. Don't assume everyone recognizes your voice.

✗ Don't make disparaging remarks about others, whether they are present or absent.

✗ Don't answer your cell phone or read email during a meeting.

✗ Pick your battles. Arguments about things that are not important will veer the meeting off track.

✗ Don't invite people who do not need to attend for the meeting to accomplish its purpose. It is inconsiderate of their time.

✗ Don't carry on side conversations during the meeting; this is rude and disrespectful to the speaker.

✗ Don't allow the discussion to wander off topic; stick to the agenda.

✗ Don't allow negativity. Meetings should address business challenges in a solution-oriented manner.

✗ If you are leading the meeting and there is not a designated secretary, have someone take notes. This frees you up to lead the meeting and provides documentation of decisions and responsibilities.

WRITTEN REPORTS

Writing is a powerful communication tool. Written reports are typically formal documentation and are archived and kept as part of the company or organization records. They often use a prescribed template for sharing data or status with upper management and boards of directors; they also provide information on the state of a project to customers and other stakeholders.

Reports should utilize correct grammar, usage, and style. To write an effective report, remember the audience and develop the document to reflect their needs. Have all reports read and reviewed by someone else; it is hard to see your own mistakes.

Sometimes stakeholders request reports because there is a problem or crisis; they may remain a requirement even after the crisis is over. Sometimes they are contractually required (by a customer) but are not useful for a given recipient. Reports need to be constantly evaluated for effectiveness, since they can require major time-consuming effort. Managers need to work with stakeholders to ensure that each report is a useful document for its intended recipients.

In the two scenarios that follow, we will explore successful and unsuccessful written reports. The first shows how a report can grow beyond its usefulness and become unwieldy. The second demonstrates a failure to create appropriate reports.

Tammy, the manager of a ten-person team, was called in to her boss's office. Jeff had just reviewed the monthly status report. He noticed there was some difficulty with a vendor/supplier and wanted additional data. Jeff requested metrics on the procurement process. Tammy spent a week gathering data. The next month, as they went into the installation and deployment phase of the project, Jeff requested detailed metrics on equipment test status and equipment installation. Tammy's team spent an additional twenty hours documenting the metrics for Jeff, and she spent thirty additional hours pulling everything together. The report had now grown to an eighty-page document that had to be updated and submitted each month. Tammy never got any feedback on the report from Jeff, and she wondered if he'd even bothered to read it.

Tammy should have talked to Jeff to see if the first report she submitted met his needs. Subsequently, Tammy should also have communicated to Jeff the amount of time and effort it took to create the report every month. Many times senior management, or customers, do not realize the effort it takes to handle their requests, and they are willing to find a more time-effective way to gather the information they need.

Tammy, the manager of a ten-person team, was called in to her boss's office. Jeff had just reviewed the monthly status report. He noticed there was some difficulty with a vendor/supplier and wanted additional data. Jeff requested metrics on the procurement process to be added to the report. Tammy told Jeff it would take a week for her to do so because they had to be manually gathered.

Jeff was surprised Tammy had to pull the metrics manually. In his last company, they had a tool that generated all the metrics he requested automatically with very little effort.

Jeff and Tammy talked about purchasing a tool to help Tammy manage her projects efficiently.

Tammy communicated to Jeff how the request would impact her work, allowing him to adjust his expectations from his old company. They created a good line of communication.

Pat, the project manager of a recently awarded contract, went through the requirements. There were thirty-six documents to deliver in the first six months, about half of which really didn't seem to have any relevance to the project. However, Pat told the team to just figure out how to develop these documents and meet the contract requirements. The team lead, Amy, did not understand why Pat didn't work with the customer to negotiate a more appropriate solution. Nevertheless, Amy and the team spent countless hours creating what she considered to be useless documentation. By the fifth month, Amy had developed a good relationship with the customer's lead engineer, Tom. Amy asked if the customer had read the delivered documents, and Tom said, "No, they're all just sitting on a shelf."

Pat was required by the contract terms to create certain documents. Pat told his team to handle written reports, even though many of them didn't make sense.

Let's look at a better way for Pat to have handled the written report requirements.

Pat, the project manager of a recently awarded contract, went through the contract requirements. There were thirty-six documents to deliver in the first six months, about half of which really didn't seem to have any relevance to the project.

Pat asked to meet with the customer's lead engineer, Tom, and showed him the analysis of the reports. Tom was willing to negotiate which documents were required and which ones to drop. He developed a new streamlined list of required written reports.

Pat's team only created the documentation on that list and was able to spend more time on the project's mission.

Pat sat down and negotiated with the customer a set of documents more appropriate to the project. This streamlined list was reasonable and appropriate; the team was grateful to Pat for negotiating the change.

The following are written report do's and don'ts:

Written Reports Do's

✓ Use correct grammar, full sentences, and proper syntax.

✓ Have the report content verified and the text proofread.

✓ Reports are typically formal documentation; they need to be accurate.

✓ Develop your report to meet the needs of the target audience.

Written Reports Don'ts

✗ Don't send in a report that has not been proofread by someone other than the writer.

✗ Don't trivialize reports; they are typically formal documentation and will probably be archived as permanent records.

✗ When using acronyms, don't assume everyone reading the document knows what they mean. Always write out the entire name on first occurrence, followed by the acronym in parentheses. Thereafter, use the acronym.

✗ Don't add more than what is necessary to the report. Include detailed backup information in an appendix, not in the main report.

SUMMARY OF COMMUNICATION TOOLS

The table below provides a brief summary of each of the communication tools we have addressed. You may use it for guidance when deciding which tool best fits your needs in a given situation, and for using that tool correctly to achieve your goals.

Communication Tool	Benefits	Disadvantages
Face-to-Face	Can see the body language, gestures, paralinguistic cues (voice, loudness, inflection, and pitch), facial expressions, and appearance. This provides feedback on how your communication is received, allowing you to adjust as needed.	It takes much more time to meet with people face-to-face.
Telephone	Easier to contact people by phone than face-to-face. With cell phones, people are typically reachable at all times of day or night. Can hear voice tones and inflection and receive feedback from the person during the communication.	Cannot see body language, gestures, or facial expressions; will miss much of how people are reacting to the message.
Emails	Easy to quickly send information to any number of people. Good for information sharing. Can be used to document decisions, policies, and actions.	No nonverbal cues, voice inflections, or tones. Very poor technique for building collaboration or carrying out confrontation.
Texting	Very quick and immediate response. Good for yes or no answers.	No nonverbal cues, voice inflections, or tones. Poor for detailed information sharing, collaboration, or confrontation.
Group Meetings	Excellent for team discussions, sharing status, or brainstorming sessions.	Should not be used for confrontation. If meetings are not run effectively, can be a time waste for the attendees.
Presentations	Typically, more formal than simple meetings. Very good for providing detailed information (such as design reviews, training). An excellent venue to provide well-thought-out communication.	Typically, longer preparation time. Should not be used for confrontation of an individual. They can waste time if not relevant to the audience.
Reports	Data sharing in a prescribed template. Excellent for information and status sharing.	Reports can become obsolete if their effectiveness is not constantly evaluated and adjustments are not made.

Chapter Summary

Each of the communication tools can be effective if used in the right setting and context but can be disastrous if used in the wrong way.

Look at your day-to-day communication.

- Are you using email or texting to deliver bad news, disparage someone, or let someone know about a performance issue?

- Do you have meetings that seem to waste people's time because there is not a clear agenda? Do you have meetings or presentations in order to confront someone?

- Are the reports you or your team generate read and used by the recipient?

Look at how you use your communication tools to ensure you are using the correct approach for each type of scenario.

Chapter 3

Using Your Communication Tools

Communication is inherently complex due to the number and diversity of pathways in which it must occur. When a project, team, or organization is in crisis, that strains communication even more. Knowing which tools will have the best impact in a given situation can dramatically affect your working relationships. In this chapter, you'll learn how to select the proper tool for the situation, taking into consideration all the personal and organizational factors that form the matrix of the communication setting.

In chapter 2 we discussed several tools: email, texting, phone conversations, face-to-face conversations, group meetings, presentations, and reports. But how to choose the right one? As the following graphic shows, three elements help a manager decide: situation, personality, and relationships.

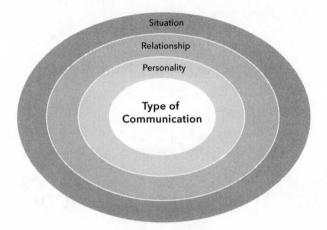

Elements of Communication

Usually, we make our decision so quickly and subconsciously that we aren't aware of these three influences. Nevertheless, we typically go through an analysis. First, we assess the situation in which the communication is to occur: Is it formal, informal, planned, unexpected, or something in between? Next, we take into account the nature of our relationship with the communication partner: a close friend, a family member, a boss, a customer, an employee? Third, we take the all-important step of recognizing the personalities involved in the transaction, both our own and the other party's. Only after moving through all three layers of the analysis are we in a position to hit the "bull's-eye"—choosing the most appropriate and effective type of communication for the purpose.

Let's take a closer look at each phase of the communication decision, considering its implications for the various methods and media we have at our disposal.

1. SITUATION

Every day we constantly communicate in verbal and nonverbal ways, making constant (and likely unconscious) adjustments for each situation. For example, if you are out at a ball game with your boss and coworkers, everyone's approach is likely more relaxed and informal than if you were giving a formal presentation to the same individuals. Context varies widely: impromptu meetings, formal presentations, technical brainstorming sessions among colleagues, scheduled weekly teleconferences, internal status meetings that occur at regular intervals, informal social gatherings of the team after work, chance hallway conversations, and everything in between. Each situation brings with it certain expectations, liabilities, and advantages, and as a manager, it is your responsibility to know how to respond appropriately.

From chapter 2, we know that there are many ways to communicate and respond in a situation. Let's take the next step of looking at real-world situations involving different communication media and discover how to apply the most effective communication tools for each.

Face-to-Face and Telephone

Face-to-face and phone conversations are very effective for one-on-one discussions, both formal and informal. Formal discussions can include performance reviews, status updates, or discussion of issues and concerns. Additionally, such meetings (preferably one-on-one) are the best tool to use for confrontation or discussing sensitive issues (chapter 15 contains detailed information and examples for confrontation techniques). Always prepare ahead of time for formal face-to-face or phone meetings.

Informal face-to-face or phone discussions fit a wide variety of situations. Both are excellent ways to form or strengthen personal connections with people or to let individuals or groups know how much you appreciate the work that they are doing. There is a popular management technique called **MBWA**—"Management by Walking Around." It's amazing how much you hear when you chat informally with others. To stay in touch with people who are not physically close, picking up the phone just to see how they are doing is just as effective and shows each person how much you care.

Email and Texting

As we learned in chapter 2, email and texting should be used only in situations where there is no controversy and where building rapport or collaboration is not the primary aim.

Having said that, realize that email can be used appropriately in both informal and formal situations. Formal examples include company or organization notices of events or deadlines, responding to a customer on a contract-related issue, responding to the board of directors, noting or resolving a supervisor's concern, or sending a communication out to the whole organization. Emails with formal content should be written in complete sentences with correct grammar, then reviewed several times by you and, if possible, by another person before sending.

Informal situations do not require such deliberate writing, but remember that email can be forwarded easily and can very quickly reach an audience you never intended to read it. If an email documents a sensitive situation, it is a good idea to mark the top and bottom of the email or the subject line indicating that it should not be forwarded or redistributed. Also, remember that sometimes the forward and reply process can generate long strings of comments, obscuring the original email's intent or, worse, reaching people never intended to receive the information. Review the entire content of the email before distribution to ensure it is appropriate for the recipients.

Texting is best between people who know each other. It should be used in informal situations for short information exchanges or yes and no questions.

To reemphasize, email and texting should not be used in situations requiring a confrontation or for discussing individual performance.

Further, they are not the best tool to use for a brainstorming or collaborative situation.

Group Meetings and Presentations

Plan meetings for situations where it is important to have a group of people together to discuss a topic. Remember what we discussed in chapter 2: all meetings should have a purpose, an agenda, and a desired outcome. Without these, meetings often waste people's time, eroding your credibility as a manager. Yet meetings—both the formal, planned variety and the less formal, last-minute meeting—can be very effective as a brainstorming, status, or collaboration technique. However, an agenda, a framework for the discussion, and a desired outcome are necessary to make sure the meeting stays on track and is focused on the correct topics.

Presentations are formal meetings where someone imparts information to a group of people, typically with handouts or information displayed on a monitor over the course of the meeting. Presentations are good for providing detailed information (such as design reviews, status reviews, and training) to an audience. To have an effective presentation, know your audience and plan around the audience's knowledge and level in the organization. For example, don't have detailed engineering information in a presentation to senior executives and vice versa. It's always a good idea to have your presentation reviewed by someone else. It's amazing how many inconsistencies, misspellings, or formatting errors a new reviewer can find. Finally, practice your presentation so you are prepared and ready.

Written Reports

Reports should be used in formal situations where information needs to be documented for contractual or legal purposes, or to provide formalized information to a group of people.

2. RELATIONSHIPS

The second element influencing the tool you choose is your relationship with the people with whom you are communicating. There are two parts to a relationship: first, formality, based on position and hierarchy within the team; second, interpersonal dynamics and trust. Formal relationships include your boss and customers; these relationships are relatively easy to identify and categorize. By contrast, interpersonal dynamics and trust are more nebulous, subject to individual interpretation and subjective judgment. Despite their less clear-cut nature, however, interpersonal components play a major role in establishing personal boundaries and intimacy levels. Knowing the social norms associated with the hierarchical nature of the relationship, as well as the mutually agreed-upon trust and intimacy levels, is vital for appropriate and effective communication.

Whether you've ever thought about it or not, you have a relationship with every person you encounter during your workday: vendors, bosses, subordinates, contractors, coworkers, customers, and others. In each relationship, the person's position, authority, and experience with respect to your own have a bearing on communication style. In addition, the intimacy level you have with each individual impacts a communication tool's effectiveness. If you have worked with your boss for twenty years and your families have a close relationship outside of work, your communication may be less formal than other people communicating with your boss in the same situation.

Regardless of the nature of the relationship, however, all business-related communication should be deliberate and mindful. Miscommunication has serious consequences: your reputation can be hurt and your relationship with another individual can be damaged. Even in casual relationships or informal communication with subordinates or support personnel, miscommunication can cause unnecessary drama and upheaval. Always remember the goal in relationships is to build up trust so that even when there is miscommunication, the other person feels comfortable enough to discuss the matter with you instead of jumping to conclusions.

Email and Texting

Texting is better used in casual relationships with less difference in hierarchy (coworkers for example). This method makes for quick and easy conversations that are more like "real time." While it is true that texting can be used in all types of relationships, much care should be taken in employing it with people in authority or who are in your formal reporting chain—either above or below you. Especially in such cases, full sentences and correct grammar should be used and the message should be thought out before sending.

Emails can be used to communicate with people in all sorts of roles. However, the type of email sent would be different if you were posing a quick question to a coworker versus making a project-related query of a customer. In all cases, emails should be proofread before sending. Much miscommunication occurs in the workplace because of hitting the "send" button too quickly. Reading your message just one more time is almost always a good idea.

Face-to-Face and Telephone

Because of the rich nonverbal context available, face-to-face conversations are the best way to judge the effectiveness of your communication. Body language and gestures demonstrate much of how someone is feeling about your relationship (see chapter 2). Many times, face-to-face meetings can become more casual and intimate as conversation progresses. Such settings can nurture relationships and build up trust so that future conversations are easier and even more informal. For all these reasons, face-to-face communication is usually the best choice if you are building a relationship, collaboration, or confrontation.

If a face-to-face meeting is not possible, calling someone on the telephone can also help build rapport. Listening to the person's words, inflections, and tone can help you modulate your communication and build trust.

Group Meetings, Presentations, and Reports

Generally, group meetings and presentations are formal. In some cases, attendees do not know each other well, and the relationship is based solely on role, responsibilities, and authority level. In these cases, communication should be deliberate and carefully planned as to content and tone, because no trust has been built up between parties. Without careful communication, attendees will make their own assumptions and judgments—which may or may not be accurate—about the people and situation.

Reports are the most formal of the communication types and, as such, are usually employed when the relationship is contractually or hierarchically based. Reports are often distributed to a broad audience with different understandings about the subject. Those reading the report may or may not have any personal relationship with those presenting it. Reports should be clear, concise, and unambiguous. It is always a good idea to have several people review the report to ensure it is clear. Naturally, reports should be drafted with proper grammar and a more formal style and should be proofread before dissemination.

3. PERSONALITY

The third and final element to consider is the personality of the persons involved—both the initiator and the receiver of the communication. In chapter 1 we discussed different models describing personality types, and in chapter 2 we covered the attributes, advantages, and disadvantages of various communication formats. As we begin to synthesize this knowledge, it's important to remember that our personality type determines how we should deliver messages and also how we prefer to receive them. Too often we assume that others prefer the communication style we find most comfortable. It is vital to realize that different people have different comfort levels with various communication styles. For example, if your boss does not like email, it will not be effective for you to send detailed emails throughout the day. The more we can adapt and utilize someone else's preferred style, the more likely it is that we will be communicating clearly and effectively.

The more you know about how to use the tools with people of different personalities, the better you will be at creating and maintaining the rapport needed to keep people on the team functioning at their best.

Email and Texting

Detailed Emailer: Some people feel very comfortable using email and tend to use this method more than face-to-face or telephone conversations. They typically have a well-managed inbox. They can be more articulate in writing than in verbal discussions. They respond well to email. However, email exchanges can get quite lengthy and detailed. They need to take care how much detail they include in emails and texts—many times these are not carefully read, especially by those people who prefer face-to-face discussions.

Short Texter or Emailer: Usually people who consistently write short emails or texts prefer face-to-face conversations or phone calls. To work with someone like this effectively, go see them in person or make a call to communicate with them. They typically are more articulate verbally and prefer to connect in person.

Email Ignorer: Two types of people do not feel pressure to read all their email. The first type is driven by interesting ideas and concepts, and an inbox full of email doesn't matter to them. The second type is the action-oriented people person for whom reading email is drudgery.

Email or texting is not effective with these types of personalities. The only way to get their attention fully is to have a face-to-face meeting or a video/phone conversation.

Face-to-Face and Telephone

The people who like face-to-face meetings crave a personal connection with people. They will want to talk after receiving a detailed email. There are several possible motivations: (1) to make sure everyone is OK; (2) to give opinion and sway people to their way of thinking; or (3) to talk out the details.

Group Meetings, Presentations, and Reports

Some people thrive on meetings; others dread them. The people who thrive in meetings may have different motivations: They may (1) like the human contact; (2) want to smooth things out; (3) want to sway others to their way of thinking; or (4) like seeing reactions when asking controversial questions.

If meetings have too much detail, the people who thrive on human contact may become disruptive by making jokes, getting up, looking at their phones, and tuning out.

Some people tune out of meetings especially if clear expectations for their participation are not set.

When it comes to reports, again, like email, you have the people who put in a lot of detail and spend a great deal of time on the report in order to make it perfect. On the other hand, some only want to show the summary and dislike the details.

Chapter Summary

Each communication event, regardless of the form of communication being used, has three elements or layers: the situation, the relationship between the parties, and the personalities of the people involved.

- Are you selecting the best communication technique for each situation?

- Are you using text or email messages for situations that require a more formal report?

- Are you using email in a confrontational situation where a face-to-face conversation would be more appropriate?

- Are you using email to get ideas from your team where a brain-storming meeting would be more effective?

- Do you have your team write formal status reports where a quick email would be more efficient?

- Do you require your team to develop formal presentations where a more informal meeting would be sufficient?

- Do you schedule face-to-face meetings to get nonconfrontational information that could easily be sent to you in an email?

Each individual has attributes that lend themselves to particular formats and styles of communication.

Building Bridges: Getting past Issues and Back on Track

When you've noted the situation, considered the nature of the relationships involved, and carefully crafted your communication for optimal reception by the personality type of your communication partner, you assume everything will go smoothly.

Of course, we all know it doesn't always work that way in the real world. So what happens when you encounter the inevitable bumps in the road—when negative circumstances, emergencies, or unanticipated difficulties cause the people you're working with to act badly?

Now that we've inventoried the communication toolbox and considered how to use it, it's time to examine what happens when, despite your best planning and forethought, things get out of kilter.

In the next section, we'll learn how to apply the principles we've learned in those difficult situations when communication is the only tool you've got to solve the problem and get the work back on track.

Part II will help give you techniques to work effectively with individuals who exhibit difficult behaviors, such as the **Manipulator**, **Gossiper**, **Naysayer**, **Controller**, **Perfectionist**, **Yes-Man**, **Drama Queen**, **Recluse**, **Whiner**, and **Liar**.

You will learn—

- To recognize and understand each of the ten different difficult behavior types.

- To understand the problems difficult behaviors bring to your team.

- The disadvantages of being or working with each personality type.

- To communicate effectively when someone is exhibiting a difficult behavior.

- To defuse the behavior and get the organization back on track by choosing the right communication tool.

No matter what difficult personalities you may encounter in your day-to-day routine—whether they originate from management, other departments in your organization, your customers, or your team members—these techniques will help you communicate effectively, purposefully, and skillfully.

Chapter 4

The Manipulator

WHO ARE THEY?

Manipulation can show up in many different ways in the workplace. It can create a toxic environment. Manipulators are often bullies who, through devious methods, control others. Manipulators often create chaotic emotional situations in order to take advantage of others.

Manipulators react due to fear: fear they are not enough, fear they are not competent. They lack respect for others and look for personality traits in others to exploit.

The person who makes up or twists situations, makes someone else look foolish, or breaks and ignores rules is often a Manipulator. They use diversion techniques to shift the conversation (usually away from their failings) and either ask questions that are not relevant or blame others for what they are not doing.

Manipulation takes many forms: withholding data, excluding certain people from communication, blaming others, and wanting credit for others' successes. Sometimes manipulation takes the form of bullying. A bully will answer questions with aggressive assertions to hide their own failings.

Following are two scenarios where a Manipulator's behavior caused major issues in an organization. In the first example, a manager caused disruption and drama, and distorted the facts in order to look good. In the second scenario, an employee was a bully and made his coworkers fearful.

Chris was concerned. He was seeing lots of finger-pointing and lack of communication between the finance team and the marketing team. Every week there was a blowup between these two groups. Chris thought all the issues had roots in the finance group, so he counseled several of the finance team members. Today a graphic artist came to him very upset because his paycheck was half the right amount; he believed the finance team shorted his pay on purpose to get back at him for a previous issue. When Chris began to reprimand the finance team, they let him know the shortfall was because of a payroll glitch that affected multiple employees, and they were frantically working to resolve it.

Chris went back to the graphic designer, who acknowledged that Simon, the marketing director, told him the finance team did it on purpose. Chris realized he had not dug deeply enough into the situation. Chris observed Simon over the next few days and realized Simon was not actually doing any of his own work. Instead he was spending his time setting up negative drama and then being consumed with it. Simon went from person to person giving them negative information about the finance team. When Chris talked to each person in the marketing department, he learned that Simon had provided different negative information to each one based on their own particular fears or issues. He also found out that Simon withheld information from the marketing team, which drove confrontations with the finance group. Simon also delegated all of his assignments to his team members and then took credit for them.

It took Chris quite a while to figure out that Simon was at the center of all the issues because the manipulation was subtle and insidious. He played the two teams off each other in a way that was sneaky and devious. Chris had given Simon information that he withheld from team members in order to create conflict.

Justin was in shock and was bewildered. He had just been reprimanded by his boss, the company's chief operating officer (COO), who had said, "Why haven't you given Kevin a staff of people and a more visible job? You are wasting a valuable talent!" A full-time member of Justin's team, Kevin was also working on a special project for his MBA. The COO served as Kevin's academic project sponsor and considered him ambitious, aggressive, and promising.

Justin had asked Kevin to perform a financial assessment and analysis on a new human resource (HR) system the company planned to install. Kevin believed this analysis would be great for his résumé and would be visible to the COO and president of the company, and so he gladly accepted. Justin thought this would be the type of visible task Kevin would like, and he walked out feeling good about the decision.

However, a few weeks later when Justin saw a draft of the analysis, he noticed it was not accurate and lacked detail. When Justin explained what was needed, Kevin lashed out, saying, "You set me up to fail by not giving me a financial analyst and other resources. You want me to fail so you can get all the glory!"

Shaken, Justin sputtered that was absolutely not the case, but Kevin stormed out and went directly to the COO.

Kevin was smart and charming, and he loved working with the COO of the company; it made him feel important. However, when Justin exposed Kevin's failings, Kevin lashed out and became a manipulative bully.

Justin did what he had done for many team members when he explained to Kevin the detail he wanted in the analysis. He had a great team and had personally mentored many of its members. He had no idea how to handle someone like Kevin.

WHAT PROBLEMS CAN A MANIPULATOR BRING TO YOUR TEAM?

A Manipulator shows the following behaviors:

- Takes discussion off track
- Blames others
- Uses or cons others
- Sets up arguments
- Makes fools of others
- Reverses position unexpectedly
- Breaks or ignores rules
- Makes up or twists situations to others' detriment
- Backstabs
- Persuades others to do negative things
- Makes inaccurate, inflammatory statements
- Sets up negative drama

A Manipulator is difficult to recognize sometimes, because they tend to be charming and persuasive but typically ignore the chain of command. A Manipulator will often pit people against each other and persuade others into negative actions. A Manipulator will often blame others and come out unscathed from a situation. Consequently, the Manipulator can be very insidious, because it is usually not obvious that the Manipulator is the cause of unrest or conflict on the team and within the whole organization.

Let's look at the two previous scenarios to see what kind of impact the Manipulator had on those around them.

In scenario one, Simon hurt the company by withholding information, setting up conflict, and taking credit for others' successes. He spent his time creating drama and then getting in the middle to cover up the fact that he was not doing any of his assignments.

In scenario two, Kevin caused dissension for his own gain. Kevin lashed out at Justin when he was feeling vulnerable and failing at a task. Instead of working with Justin and taking his comments as a way to grow, Kevin manipulated the COO to create conflict and make Justin look bad. This wasted time and hurt the unity of the team.

The following are some disadvantages of being or working with a Manipulator:

- Manipulators have a strong tendency to look after their own interests without regard to the team. Consequently, others may not see them as team players or may consider them untrustworthy.

- Manipulators will expect others to fend for themselves. This can lead to the team feeling resentful and abandoned during difficult phases.

- Manipulators spend a lot of time and energy creating an environment where they can control the outcome. Many times it is difficult to know the extent to which the Manipulator is damaging the team.

- Manipulators will create unnecessary drama to deflect any negative comments (e.g., performance issues). Such drama can quickly destroy team unity and derail an organization.

- Manipulators tend to think the rules don't apply to them. Setting appropriate boundaries can be a challenge with this type of person.

HOW CAN YOU COMMUNICATE EFFECTIVELY WITH MANIPULATORS?

First, don't let the Manipulator control your attention and emotions. Be aware how you are reacting and how the Manipulator is affecting you. Don't stoop to the Manipulator's level—stop gossiping about them, don't react in a negative way, and don't resort to manipulating back or taking any type of revenge.

A healthy relationship is about trust and honesty. When you notice you are being manipulated, don't cower or ignore the other person's words and actions. Gently but honestly point out your view or your opinion.

When the Manipulator is your customer or your boss, set up ways to ask direct but open-ended questions to get at the heart of issues. Remember, a Manipulator is coming from a place of fear, so confronting them directly will cause them to be defensive and attack you.

If the Manipulator is a team member, give the Manipulator a way to achieve success so they can work on new patterns of behavior. Reward behaviors that build trust and unity. Have compassion and understand that deep down they are worried or scared.

If a Manipulator does not feel wanted or is not in the middle of the action, they will create controversy; you must come up with ways to keep the Manipulator's energies constructively engaged.

Above all, don't gossip with or about the Manipulator, don't engage with the Manipulator's bad behavior, and keep control. You will be amazed how much easier it is to communicate effectively with a Manipulator when your emotions are not in the way.

HOW DO YOU DISARM A MANIPULATOR?

Manipulators are controlling, so it is critical to remove some of that control in a positive way. Ask probing questions that point out that they are only looking at the picture from one side. For example: Can you help me understand how this benefits the program?

With bullies, remain firm. Call their bluff by gently and calmly exposing the fallacies in their statements. Use a direct, no-nonsense approach to reveal their deceptions. The bully has achieved their goal if you get flustered or rattled.

Don't become their victim. We are manipulated because we allow it; and refusing to be manipulated is the first step. In order to not get sucked into a manipulative conversation, try these techniques:

- Delay the conversation or the decision. Use words like "Let me think about it"; "Let me get back to you."

- Stop talking, and stop gossiping. When you turn into a gossip or complainer, you are only hurting yourself. You are giving the Manipulator ammunition to hurt you and control you. They will twist your words against you.

- Stop reacting. Don't get sucked into their drama. Stay unemotional. Your emotions will make you seem weak to a Manipulator, and they will feed off those weaknesses.

If someone has manipulated you and identified himself or herself as untrustworthy, you need to understand that and act accordingly. Change your communication techniques around the Manipulator. Be factual, crisp, and brief. Be honest and point out inconsistencies in their statements. Above all, don't give the Manipulator the satisfaction of seeing you react emotionally.

Take responsibility for your part in the manipulation. You have allowed yourself to be manipulated by not setting boundaries, by getting sucked into their drama, or by engaging with them in a negative way. Stop worrying about how they feel and stop trying to fix them.

The following are techniques for working with a Manipulator:

- Don't react to a Manipulator, but firmly, calmly, and honestly state your point of view.

- Keep the Manipulator engaged and busy so they have less time and energy to manipulate.

- Keep seeing the big picture, and don't get caught up in your emotions.

- Reward the Manipulator's behavior that is constructive and unifying.

WHAT TYPE OF COMMUNICATION TOOLS WORK THE BEST FOR A MANIPULATOR?

Face-to-Face and Telephone:

Face-to-face or phone conversations can be effective in working with a Manipulator if you use a direct, factual approach to expose any deception.

A Manipulator thrives on face-to-face conversations. They can set up arguments, blame others, or provide inaccurate statements. When you meet with a Manipulator, do not allow them to make you angry or defensive. After every meeting with a Manipulator, document your conversation and send it to the Manipulator in a written form (i.e., email) so both of you have a record of the conversation.

Email and Text:

Email can be effective when working with a Manipulator as long as the emails are precise and clear so that the information is not up for interpretation. Texting is not recommended unless you can limit yourself to short, nonconfrontational answers.

Meetings and Presentations:

Meeting and presentations are effective when working with a Manipulator. It is more difficult for a Manipulator to twist the truth in a group setting. The meeting must be run with an agenda, boundaries need to be set, everyone must be clear on the information and direction from the meeting. It is also important to send out minutes from the meeting with the resulting decisions and actions. This will reduce the misinterpretation and inaccurate statements from the Manipulator.

Written Reports:

Written reports are also good for Manipulators. With the information written down, typically in a specific format focusing on facts, it makes it more difficult to manipulate. Let's look at the two prior scenarios to see what could be done to create a different outcome.

> Chris needed to make all the manipulation visible and to defuse the drama. He set up a weekly meeting with the finance team and the marketing department, including Simon. At each meeting he addressed the issues that had come to light in the previous week. He told the finance manager and marketing director to come to him directly if there were any problems. The first week was contentious with a good deal of mistrust on each side, but after some issues were resolved fairly and quickly, the meetings became productive.

Chris also had a one-on-one with Simon, during which he outlined all the manipulation he had seen and told Simon he needed him to solve problems and not create them. Chris sent him to training for knowledge Simon needed for his job and then monitored him closely. Chris kept an eye out for any withholding of information, blaming others, taking credit for their work, and not doing his assignments. The honest conversation gave Simon an opportunity to own his behavior and change it.

In the weekly meetings, Chris brought to light all the issues and underlying mistrust. He created a forum for the teams to start working together, build relationships, and trust one other. He also addressed Simon directly about his manipulation. Chris realized that some of the underlying reason for Simon's behavior was he didn't have knowledge to do his job. Chris sent Simon to a training class to help remedy that knowledge gap. Chris also monitored Simon closely so the manipulative behaviors didn't come back.

Justin realized that he had exposed a weakness in Kevin that caused a negative reaction. Justin put together a plan to have a financial analyst work with Kevin and train him on his knowledge gaps. He informed the financial analyst that she should not do all of Kevin's work for him but should mentor and train him. Justin then went to the COO and explained the plan to help Kevin complete the analysis. Justin also offered to work with the COO to develop a career path plan for Kevin. Finally, he made sure the COO knew that Kevin manipulated the situation but that Justin planned to work with him to provide support and help him grow.

Justin had to figure out a positive way to work with Kevin and to repair his relationship with the COO. He provided the support Kevin needed to be successful. He involved the COO in the plan to support Kevin's professional growth.

Chapter Summary

Manipulators show up in many different ways and create a harmful environment. At their worst, they are controlling bullies, creating a chaotic emotional environment allowing them to exploit others. Remember, Manipulators are reacting to their own fear: fear they are not enough, fear they are not competent.

- Have you had to work with someone who is a Manipulator? What was the impact the Manipulator had on you and the team?

- What could you have done differently to work with the Manipulator successfully? How could you have disarmed the Manipulator?

- Have you been a Manipulator by withholding data, not including certain people in communications, blaming others, or taking credit for others' success? How do think that makes others feel? How can you change your behavior?

Refusing to be manipulated is the first step. Remember, if we are manipulated, it is because we allow it. With Manipulators, use a direct, no-nonsense approach to reveal their deceptions. The bully has achieved their goal if you get flustered or rattled. Don't become their victim.

Chapter 5

The Gossiper

WHO ARE THEY?

Gossip is rampant in most workplaces. People speculate about everything: a reorganization, if their coworker will get fired, how much money others make, the future of the company, who slighted whom, what employees are doing in their life outside of work, employee relationships, and personal gripes about others.

There is benign gossip, which is an exchange of information. However, this chapter deals with the kind that hurts others. Negative gossip can create a toxic culture where employees don't trust one another and morale drops. You need to act on gossip if it disrupts the workplace, causing morale issues or hurting employees.

People gossip for a variety of reasons:

- The Gossiper finds negative comments an easy way to bond with others.

- The Gossiper has anxiety around their social position and needs to establish themselves in the group.
- The Gossiper feels powerful with knowledge that others don't have.
- The Gossiper feels better putting others down.
- The Gossiper wants to have interesting things to say to be the center of attention.
- The Gossiper wants to hurt people they envy.

Let's look at two scenarios where a Gossiper's behavior harms the organization. In the first scenario, a department manager spreads rumors about people in another department, hurting their morale. The second scenario shows a customer attacking an individual employee.

Yolanda was walking down the hall and saw Frank, the leader of a large department, coming out of an office. She knew people listened to him and considered what he said to be true even if it wasn't. As she watched, he entered another employee's office. Frank was gossiping about something!

Later that afternoon, Yolanda noticed there was a lot of chatter in the hallways that stopped when she walked by. She wondered what terrible things Frank was saying about her now. He had pushed out Kim, a good worker, after she turned him down for a date. Subsequently, Frank took every opportunity to say negative and disrespectful things about Kim.

Frank was masterful, sounding sincere and honest while talking about people behind their backs. The organization suffered distrust and unnecessary drama as a result of Frank's actions, and yet somehow their boss liked and protected him. Yolanda had previously approached their boss, who dismissed her claim, saying Frank was a good guy. She had met with Frank yesterday and told him to stop talking about two of her employees, but he denied any wrongdoing. He lashed out at her, saying, "You're full of shit! You're too sensitive." She was sure he was retaliating by talking about her now. Yolanda knew she had to do something to stop his gossiping.

In the scenario above, Frank probably had a number of reasons why he targeted others for gossip. Frank felt powerful in the belief that he knew something other people didn't. Frank liked when he was the center of attention and people listened to him.

Marty had a great team. They were hardworking, well respected by customers, had fun together, and had become a close-knit group. Pete, a client rep, would come over in the afternoon to "check on things." Really he was just gossiping. It started out with comments about his boss and others in his organization. People listened to him at first to get information about the client organization. Then it started to get more personal. Marty noticed that Pete started talking a lot about one person in particular, Mike. Mike was very smart but sometimes had a hard time articulating his ideas. Pete started using the nickname "Muddling Mike" for the way he struggled to talk. Marty noticed that his team had started to isolate Mike and didn't talk to him very much. Mike would come in, sit in his cube, and just look miserable all day. Today, Marty heard Pete say another team member dressed geeky. Marty had to stop Pete from harming his team further and to pull them back together again.

In this second scenario, a customer, Pete, disrupted team unity. He had already isolated one person and was starting on another.

WHAT PROBLEMS CAN GOSSIPERS BRING TO YOUR TEAM?

A Gossiper shows the following behaviors:

- A Gossiper can target specific people because they perceive them as weak (having a characteristic that is an easy target) or because they were slighted by the person.

- A Gossiper will use his words to put someone down to look better by comparison.

- A Gossiper will say negative things to connect with others. It is easy to get people's attention when you have some interesting gossip.

- A Gossiper sometimes will talk about someone they envy so they are "cut down to size."

- A Gossiper can also take true information and exaggerate it to make it more interesting but in the process hurt someone.

Most people want to learn more about the people in their organization. This curiosity can feed the Gossiper to find more things to talk about, even if not true, so they can be connected, be the center, and feel superior.

Gossipers are detrimental to your team regardless of their position or role. When gossip becomes the norm, people polarize into factions.

The following are disadvantages of being or working with a Gossiper:

- A Gossiper's negative connection with people can be contagious, and the organization can deteriorate into either polarized teams or isolated individuals that don't communicate or trust each other at all.

- A Gossiper's comments can fuel conflict and mistrust between people.

- A Gossiper can reduce productivity by diverting focus to emotional drama instead of work.

- A Gossiper is typically not popular because they are not trusted.

- Sometimes the gossip can spread like the telephone game; each person embellishes a little and the information becomes more and more damaging.

In the first scenario, Frank was disruptive to Yolanda's team, and now he was targeting Yolanda personally. In the second scenario, the customer, Pete, started breaking apart a close-knit and productive team.

HOW CAN YOU COMMUNICATE EFFECTIVELY WITH GOSSIPERS?

Gossiping behavior is all about the individual's perceived social status. They may feel a need to bond with others, and nothing is better at doing that than shared secrets. The Gossiper may feel better when putting others down, or wants the attention, or feels powerful having knowledge that others do not have.

First, look at yourself! Sometimes people gossip because of a lack of information from their leadership. When people lack information, they fill in the blanks—usually in a negative way. Are you providing enough information to the workforce so they are comfortable? If there is regular, open communication across the organization, it will reduce the fodder the Gossiper will have. Make sure you are not gossiping—you need to model the behavior you want to see in the workplace.

When communicating with a Gossiper, please keep in mind that they may feel anxious about their place in the organization. It is better to use a coaching approach to the situation—it is a habit the person needs to break. Use a nonconfrontational tone that makes it clear you believe the gossip is negative. The person may or may not understand the harm that's being done.

Never send out an email blast about gossiping, as it's not effective. It can backfire and actually make it seem like you are not taking care of the problem directly. In general, email is not an appropriate way to handle any employee issue.

Speak up directly to the Gossiper if you hear talk in a group or individually, using phrases like—

- "Wow, I don't think that is true."

- "That's not my impression."

- "Let's go ask our boss if he can provide us with more information."

- "I'd rather not discuss him without him being here."

- "I think she is doing a great job."

At a minimum, change the conversation immediately so the gossip doesn't take hold. This will shut down the Gossiper and steer the conversation from the gossipy topics.

Using these techniques in front of others gives the whole team ways to stop the gossip and provides them an alternative way to understand the information.

HOW DO YOU DISARM A GOSSIPER?

Gossiping can be addictive, and it is not an easy habit to break. Like any other habit, when it is removed, it needs to be replaced by something else. A Gossiper needs to be part of the team in a positive way. Help the Gossiper to be more of a team player by teaching him or her to replace negative comments with positive, good gossip (saying good things about people). Keep the Gossiper focused on teamwork and positive statements.

Meet with the whole team, not singling anyone out, and discuss the difference between positive gossip and negative gossip. Encourage positive talk. For example, in your staff meeting or at the start of any meeting or even just in the hallways, mention the accomplishments of individuals: "Suzie just found a new client"; "Tom did a great job planning the picnic—it should be really fun." You could even go as far as going around the room in your staff meeting and having everyone say one positive thing about one other person.

Techniques for working with a Gossiper include the following:

- Give attention to positive stories.

- Shut down negative statements.

- Make sure they feel they are part of the team.

- Provide detailed company information so the Gossiper doesn't have a way to fill in the blanks with negative gossip.

WHAT TYPE OF COMMUNICATION TOOLS WORK THE BEST FOR A GOSSIPER?

Face-to-Face and Telephone:

Gossipers thrive on face-to-face conversations. It gives them the chance to share secrets and feel superior. When you meet with a Gossiper, do not get sucked into any gossip during your conversation. Keep to the facts. Stop any gossiping immediately by focusing the conversation on positive information.

Email and Text:

Email and texting can be effective when working with a Gossiper, as long as the emails are factual without any controversial information or information that could fuel gossip.

Meetings and Presentations:

Meetings and presentations are extremely effective when working with a Gossiper. Group discussions do not allow the Gossiper to move from person to person. Everyone hears the same information. It is always a good practice to summarize the meeting discussion and actions at the end to make sure everyone has heard the same information. This reduces the ammunition the Gossiper has to talk negatively about topics.

Written Reports:

Written reports are a good way to communicate to Gossipers. Reports are typically precise and concise without providing avenues to gossip.

Let's pick up with the scenarios, with Yolanda and Marty being more effective in handling their Gossipers.

Yolanda went home that night and thought about the situation with Frank. She knew that people like to hear the titillating negative gossip, and it made Frank the center of attention. She wanted to develop a better relationship with him and focus his conversation on good things to say instead of negative.

The next day Yolanda went into Frank's office and shut the door so they could have a private conversation. She told him she was sorry she yelled at him yesterday and that she was just being protective of her team. Yolanda then told Frank a list of great things her team had done, both at work and on their free time. She had worked hard on the list last night and was able to identify twenty interesting facts about her team. Things like: Mary was a world-ranked ice skater when she was young; Bobbie had saved the company $5M dollars by automating testing processes; Tina had played field hockey in college and was in the national championship one year; Jay volunteered in a local homeless shelter every weekend; and so on.

Frank was speechless for a few seconds and then said he had no idea her team had done so many cool things.

Yolanda walked out feeling that her list gave Frank some good things to say about people. She made it a point every week to advertise some interesting facts about the people on her team, and the whole company looked forward to it.

Yolanda was able to get Frank to start focusing his chatter on more positive items and, in the process, got the whole company focused on all the good and interesting things her team has done.

Marty first needed to pull the team together and then figure out how to deal with Pete. Marty asked Mike out to lunch. He wanted to make sure Mike knew he was a valuable and respected member of the team. They had a good conversation. Marty told Mike how important he was and that he knew Pete had not been kind to him. Mike looked as if he was going to cry. He had been keeping all the pain bottled up. Mike then opened up a bit and said he thought he'd solved a difficult engineering issue. He had been afraid to say anything because the others might make fun of his unusual way of approaching the problem. At the next staff meeting, Marty highlighted Mike's accomplishments and the engineering solution he'd come up with. Marty also took his whole team bowling one afternoon (something he knew Mike was good at) so the team would have fun together again.

Marty also approached Pete. He knew he needed to get the customer focused on the project and not on the people. Marty said that he would like Pete's interactions with his team to be more formalized and done in meetings. Whenever Pete was in the building, Marty stayed close by so he could keep Pete's discussions on the work.

Marty actively worked to bring his team back together and make sure the person who was targeted by negative gossip, Mike, knew he was valued. Marty then limited the customer's informal time with his team to limit the gossiping.

Chapter Summary

Gossip is disruptive to a workplace and can create an environment with low morale and lack of trust. People gossip for a variety of reasons, and Gossipers may or may not know the harm they are doing to the organization or to individuals. Gossiping can be contagious in an organization, causing people to connect in a negative way.

- What immediate steps can you take to reduce the gossip within your team?
- How can you disarm the Gossiper?
- Have you ever gossiped and felt regret because the gossip was destructive to another person?
- How have you felt when you found out someone gossiped about you?

Replace negativity with good talk. Keep the Gossiper focused on teamwork and positive statements.

Chapter 6

The Naysayers

WHO ARE THEY?

Naysayers say why things cannot or should not be done. They have strong opinions, and they question every decision. Naysayers focus on the flaws of the situation.

Let's look at two scenarios where a Naysayer's behavior hurts an organization. In the first scenario, a Naysayer takes over the discussion, and no one can figure out how to defuse her. The second scenario shows a project manager's boss as a Naysayer who throws the whole project into chaos.

> Elizabeth, the new director of a homeless women's shelter, was walking to her first board meeting. The agenda included a large fundraising project. Last year, the shelter had not raised nearly enough to cover its operating expenses, forcing them to dip into their meager savings account. Elizabeth was excited and had some innovative ideas for raising the necessary funds.

Elizabeth, stepping into the room, smiled broadly at everyone. Linda, the president of the volunteer board, sat with her arms crossed and just glared at Elizabeth. Linda was always so negative and irritating; everything out of her mouth seemed to start with the words "In the past we . . ." or "You should do it this way . . ." Elizabeth had ignored Linda on multiple occasions and continued to do so now. Elizabeth passed around handouts describing her new approach and started an impassioned discussion about her ideas.

Linda interrupted Elizabeth in mid-sentence, saying, "These ideas will never work. They're worthless, and we need to go back to the way the fundraising has always been handled." Linda started listing all the problems with Elizabeth's plan.

Elizabeth was startled by this outburst and didn't know what to say. Everyone in the room seemed to shrink down while Linda continued her tirade. Linda then abruptly changed the subject, saying they had other business to attend to, and dismissed Elizabeth from the meeting. No other board member said a word. Elizabeth got up, gathered her papers, and walked in a daze back to her office.

Naysayers have a strong commitment to and belief in their goals. They value people who listen to their beliefs. If they believe their ideas will not be considered, they are disruptive and discount others' opinions.

In the scenario above, ignoring Linda had thrown her into a defensive posture and escalated her bad behavior. Linda had been an original founding member of the shelter, working tirelessly to get it started. For years following the shelter's inception, Linda had been the driving force in making sure the organization met its mission to homeless women. She attacked Elizabeth because she felt that Elizabeth did not respect her opinion. She felt that Elizabeth, a new director, was threatening to undermine all she had built up over the years.

Annette threw a folder down on her desk, frustrated that the construction manager, Paul, wasn't setting up the build schedule for the new community center as it should be. She walked into the planning meeting and told the entire leadership team why the project would fail and then proceeded to list everything the team had done wrong. Annette yelled at Paul in front of them and walked out. The energy in the room deflated, with everyone staring at each other in silence.

Paul rolled his eyes as Annette walked out; her tirades were frequent. He had tried to tell Annette that yelling was harmful to the team, but she was so sensitive to criticism that she just lashed out. Though Paul did his best, it was becoming increasingly harder to keep morale up. Everyone was working a lot of hours and starting to show signs of fatigue. They had started complaining. He had heard through the grapevine that his most valuable team member was looking for a new job. Paul started thinking that maybe he needed a new job too.

Annette obviously wanted Paul and the team to recognize her expertise and listen to her advice. When Paul did not respect her opinions and follow her instructions, she escalated her rigidity and began preaching at them. She did not trust Paul or his team and was very critical of everything they did.

Before looking at how Elizabeth or Paul could handle the situation better, let's look at why Naysayers act the way they do.

WHAT PROBLEMS CAN NAYSAYERS BRING TO YOUR TEAM?

A Naysayer shows the following behaviors:

- Crusades or preaches

- Acts self-righteous (finds faults with others)
- Expresses rigidity about "my way" or "the right way"
- Is sarcastic and critical
- Focuses on what is wrong instead of what is right

The Naysayer's attitude can be catching, and your team will often start becoming polarized; others will either be drawn to or repelled by the negative attitude. Team members may start avoiding working with others because of the strong negative energy. Team members may get ill, feel burned out, or become less productive.

In the first scenario, Linda's behavior was difficult for the other board members. They respected her efforts on behalf of the shelter and didn't want to alienate her. Unfortunately, when Linda was challenged—or believed she was being challenged—she became very opinionated and refused to listen to anyone else. All the members felt sorry for Elizabeth, but they didn't know how to help her. One member was thinking about quitting the board because Linda's behavior caused him a lot of stress; he always felt ill after any encounter with her.

In the second scenario, Annette threw the project into chaos. Her Naysayer behavior was detrimental to the functioning of the team. First of all, the team members didn't understand why Paul let Annette treat him so badly. Further, now that she was starting to attack them, the whole team was demoralized. Their unresponsiveness led Annette to escalate, leaving her angry and unproductively focused only on what she perceived was wrong.

Disadvantages of being or working with a Naysayer include the following:

- Naysayers are opinionated and can be resistant to innovative ideas or creative solutions.

- A Naysayer sees themselves as right and others as wrong; there is little or no middle ground. This can create a sense of separation from the team. If Naysayers have social or political influence, they may recruit others to join in their point of view and create a divisive environment.

- A Naysayer can waste the time and energy of others who try to introduce useful ideas or move the team in a needed new direction. The Naysayer can be seen as a liability to innovation and forward motion.

- The Naysayer's negative thinking can be contagious, particularly when people are stressed or there is already an element of dissension among the team members.

- Naysayers may try to subconsciously sabotage workable solutions in order to save face and be proved right in their opinions.

- If a Naysayer is particularly vocal in their opinions, team members may feel their perspective is not valued or appreciated and resent having to work with the Naysayer.

HOW CAN YOU COMMUNICATE EFFECTIVELY WITH THE NAYSAYER?

Naysayers want to feel they have been heard. If you ignore them or marginalize them, they will only become louder and more disruptive. Sometimes the Naysayer will stay in an organization or project that is not going the way they want, even if they have good opportunities elsewhere, because the Naysayer wants to prove that they are right.

It is much better to deal with a Naysayer in person one-on-one than with any other communication method. Going head-to-head with a Naysayer in a group meeting or through email will just escalate the situation. A Naysayer comes across as blustery and strong but is typically very sensitive and has a deep need to be right. Thanking them at the end of meetings can help them feel respect.

When talking to a Naysayer, keep the discussion on the facts and stay away from your opinions. Listen to their view of the facts. Try to use words that do not convey emotions or judgments. Many times, Naysayers have good ideas, but their approach is disruptive. When Naysayers are backed into a corner, they dig in and stop listening. Provide the Naysayers with a safe place to discuss their opinions and the facts of the situation; give them face-saving opportunities to change their minds without feeling any outside judgment.

When a Naysayer is your boss or customer, be very careful when challenging their opinion; they will most likely go on the offensive. Naysayers typically do have well-thought-out opinions, but their delivery is sometimes tough to handle. Try to meet with a Naysayer or customer in person and one-on-one as much as possible. If a Naysayer sees a weakness, they will press the attack, so be very prepared and have metrics and facts to support the discussion. A Naysayer as your boss or customer needs to know you are committed to the organization's success, so keep discussion focused on tasks. They typically do not want a lot of small talk, because it both wastes their time and shows them you are not as focused on the organization as they might wish.

When a Naysayer is a team member or a member of a supporting organization, meet with him or her individually to listen and calm any anger. Naysayers are disruptive in meetings and cause other team members to shut down if they are allowed to talk unchecked. Set up your meetings and discussions to be very organized and structured, giving everyone a turn to talk, and include time limits. Give Naysayers a way to "save face." Their bad behavior will escalate if their opinions are ignored or even shown to be wrong.

HOW DO YOU DISARM A NAYSAYER?

Keep a Naysayer focused on facts to reduce their tendency to push beliefs on others. A Naysayer performs better when around others who share high standards of integrity, dependability, and trust.

Techniques for working with a Naysayer include the following:

- Let them know what you admire or respect about them.

- Keep the discussions around the facts and the tasks at hand.

- Listen to their perspective, and repeat specific points you are willing to look at further.

- Make sure your meetings are structured with time limits for each topic.

- Shut down the Naysayer if the conversation starts escalating into finger-pointing.

- Appoint the Naysayer to an important decision-making committee.

- Ask for the Naysayer's perspective in staff meetings.

- Encourage the Naysayer to make suggestions to the appropriate persons regarding ideas for the organization's improvement.

WHAT TYPE OF COMMUNICATION TOOLS WORK THE BEST FOR A NAYSAYER?

Face-to-Face and Telephone:

Face-to-face and telephone conversations with a Naysayer can be very effective if you listen to their concerns and do not get defensive. A Naysayer wants to be heard; if they are ignored, the negative attitude typically escalates.

Email and Text:

Email and texting can be effective when working with a Naysayer, as long as the emails are factual without any controversial information or information that could fuel the Naysayer. If emails become negative, preachy, or full of emotion, stop responding immediately and go talk to the person face-to-face.

Meetings and Presentations:

Meetings and presentations can be challenging when working with a Naysayer. Naysayers will be disruptive because they preach and focus on the negative. If there is anything controversial on the agenda, it is better to meet with the Naysayer beforehand to work out their concerns so they will not be disruptive.

Written Reports:

Written reports are good for Naysayers as long as the report is well written without any controversial information. Request the Naysayer to review the report and provide any comments in written form before the report is finalized. Take into account all the Naysayer's comments before the final report is issued.

Let's look at scenarios with Elizabeth and Paul being more effective in handling their Naysayers.

After the meeting, Elizabeth knew she needed to get Linda more comfortable with the idea of a new director at the shelter. She set up a meeting with Linda and asked for her perspectives. Elizabeth listened to Linda talk about the shelter's history and all that she had done to keep it going, year after year. Elizabeth thanked Linda for her hard work and said how much she respected Linda for being so dedicated and working so hard. Near the end of the meeting, Elizabeth told Linda that she wanted to know her opinion about how to help increase fundraising for the current year. Elizabeth slowly interjected her ideas into the conversation. Linda responded warmly and got excited about the new approach.

Elizabeth asked Linda if she wanted to present the new ideas to the board. Elizabeth and Linda walked into the board meeting together and Linda presented the ideas with enthusiasm.

Elizabeth disarmed Linda by valuing her opinion and recognizing her dedication to the homeless shelter. Elizabeth did not allow her ego to get in the way, and she let Linda present the ideas to the board. She made Linda an ally instead of an enemy.

Paul knew he needed to do something to change his relationship with Annette, or the whole project would fall apart. He also recognized he needed to listen to the ideas and not the delivery method, especially since he found Annette's abrasive, opinionated tone off-putting. He set up a meeting for the next day. He spent the evening thinking about the tasks Annette wanted to implement on the project and listed each one he felt they could try. He then listed some that he really didn't want to do but thought he could include without harm to the project. Paul was surprised the final list of things he didn't think they could do was very small. He wanted to make sure he showed Annette he was willing to listen and implement her opinions, so he prepared a script for their conversation and practiced it several times. He then steeled himself and walked in to see Annette. Paul told Annette he wanted to improve their relationship and he wanted to talk about her ideas. Paul brought out the list of implementable ideas. He said, "You have good opinions. Could we meet for fifteen minutes, three times a week, and share opinions on the project?" The conversation went much better than Paul could have imagined; Annette was willing to talk about every item on the list. She was impressed that Paul respected her enough to actually listen to her. She agreed to meet three times a week.

Paul listened to Annette and recognized that her opinions had value that was not affected by her way of delivering them. He was able to negotiate tasks for the team to accomplish. Annette was happy that Paul listened to her, and she started feeling better. She was looking forward to the frequent meetings with Paul.

Chapter Summary

Naysayers focus on the flaws of the situations and state why things cannot or should not be done. They want to be heard, and when marginalized, they typically get more disruptive. They want to be respected.

- What impact have you felt when you had someone around you who was negative and found fault in everything?
- What can you do differently when you have a Naysayer around you?
- Have you caught yourself being negative and always pointing out what could go wrong? How do you think that impacted others around you?

When talking to a Naysayer, keep to the facts, and use words that do not convey emotions, judgments, or opinions. Often Naysayers have good ideas or are pointing out an important issue. Take the time to listen to the Naysayer and find the idea or issue behind all the blustery words.

Chapter 7

The Controller

WHO ARE THEY?

Controllers want things done the "right way" . . . and of course the right way to do, act, think, and speak is their way. They are interested not just in the outcome but how you get to the end goal. Controllers are motivated by power and exercising influence over others. They don't delegate well and get frustrated quickly. Controllers rely on domination to feel safe and confident.

A Controller and a non-Controller may seek the same outcome, but the Controller makes the job harder by specifying how others should behave. Typically, that backfires by making it harder for people to accomplish the goal.

Controllers do not respect people the way they are. They give unwanted advice, interfere so others do things the "right way," and obsess on the specifics of how things happen. Controllers have a high level of internal chaos and anxiety. The outward control is a way to guard against their own vulnerability.

At the extreme, controlling people are narcissists. A narcissist is self-centered, lacks empathy, is arrogant, and craves admiration. A narcissist rarely listens, is quick to blame others, and is a bully. Narcissists inflate their contributions and importance.

Below are two scenarios. In the first example the Controller is a boss micromanaging her staff. In the second, a new CEO of a company has a controlling staff member.

Eve walked out of work feeling very frustrated. She loved her job, her teammates, and the short commute, but she was not sure she could take one more day working for Neal. He wanted to be copied on every single email she sent out. Today he told his whole staff that they weren't allowed to talk to people in other departments without him there. Eve had to talk to different people across the company twenty times a day. This new mandate was crazy.

Eve hit her limit today when Neal said, in front of her peers, that she wasn't doing her job and he didn't know why she worked for the company. His comment was based on one task she did not complete because she did not know how Neal wanted it done. Neal had said he wanted his team to work independently, but when anyone tried, he bullied them and made them do it over again the exact way he prescribed. Even though Eve was experienced, Neal would not let her make any decisions on her own. The result was lower productivity from Eve because she had to get his approval on every decision she wanted to make.

Controllers need everything done their way and want to be part of every decision and every conversation, because they have a need to know everything that is happening. In this example, Neal leverages his controlling behavior across his entire team, affecting productivity and trust.

> Jay had a dilemma. He had just taken over a large organization and was assessing all of his direct reports. He held one-on-ones with over forty employees. Everyone complained that Sally, a director, was mean and controlling. Sally had a hard time delegating, and when she did delegate, it was very small, specific tasks that she expected to be completed before assigning the next one. Sally was impatient and cruel to the people who didn't do the task the way she wanted it done. It also came out that Sally did her job very well and had fixed many problems when she first came in. Unfortunately, Jay's team had hit their limit of her bullying. There had been and continued to be a lot of attrition in the organization, with Sally's unreasonableness as the primary reason given.

Controllers harm the organization by being rigid, not delegating, and being impatient. Sally is very competent and skilled. She has helped the company in the past. However, she feels attacked as her power and influence wane, causing an acceleration of her controlling behavior.

WHAT PROBLEMS CAN A CONTROLLER BRING TO YOUR TEAM?

A Controller will show the following characteristics:

- Takes over groups
- Tells others what to do and how to do it
- Does not delegate well or delegates small, specific tasks

- Insists they know what is best for people
- Wants things done their way

It is difficult to work with a Controller, especially when they are stressed, because they become very rigid, don't allow any freedom in how the task gets done, and tend to have very narrow vision.

Controllers are goal oriented and typically work hard, but they can hurt morale and creativity.

In the first scenario, Eve's productivity and morale was much lower than it should have been because of Neal's controlling behavior. Eve was not allowed to make any decision, and everything she did had to be the exact way her boss wanted it to be done. The company would probably lose a valuable employee.

In the second scenario, Sally's controlling was harming the whole company. She was not empowering her team but micromanaging them. The extreme controlling got Sally what she needed in the short term, but it was holding the company back and sabotaging both individual and company growth.

The disadvantages of working with a Controller include the following:

- Controllers not only tell people what to do but how to do it, irritating people and causing work to be slower.

- Controllers also want to be part of all decisions, which creates bottlenecks.

- Controllers delegate only small, specific tasks so they keep complete control over the process, disempowering people in the organization.

- Controllers create disruptive communications because they are critical and nit-pick, reducing morale.

- Controllers tend to get more controlling when stress is high, causing more stress in the organization.

HOW CAN YOU COMMUNICATE EFFECTIVELY WITH CONTROLLERS?

Provide details to Controllers to help lower anxiety levels. Do not respond with emotion to their controlling. Do not take it personally. Their control compulsion is not about you. The less you react to their incitements, the more objective you can be. If you feel upset and can't continue in a conversation objectively, then buy yourself some time and step out. Say things like, "Let me get back to you," or "Let me think about it," or "Let's finish talking about this tomorrow."

Do not expect to please Controllers. You will never to do the work to their level of expectation. Instead, make it a point to give praise and recognize their contributions to the workplace.

Controllers typically see things as black and white—things are good or bad, right or wrong. Put things in writing so you can be clear and concise and protect yourself from sabotage and so expectations are clear on both sides. Keep copies of all your interactions. You might want to keep a log of any conversations.

Stand up to a Controller without being confrontational. They do not react well to a direct challenge. Stay calm and controlled while talking to a Controller.

When your subordinate is a Controller, make a point of recognizing his work achievements and accomplishments. For Controllers, accomplishments and domination are more highly regarded than relationships, so monitor team dynamics to make sure Controllers do not alienate themselves or foster resentment.

If you work for a Controller boss, be sure to thank him or her for their help and leadership on any given project. Keep communications short, accurate, and to the point. Provide consistent, factual, and regular updates on how things are going.

Recognize the efforts of Controller coworkers. When working together, communicate with them clearly and concisely. Remember not to assume they will delegate responsibility very well.

HOW DO YOU DISARM A CONTROLLER?

To keep a Controller working at his best, compliment his accomplishments. Keep a Controller focused on their own achievement—it is important to recognize their accomplishments and thank them. You need to build trust with a Controller by accomplishing a goal that is important to them, on time and with high quality. A Controller is insecure; controlling others makes them feel safe and secure.

Techniques for working with a Controller include the following:

- Thank the Controller for meeting deadlines.

- Make a point to recognize accomplishments and dedication.

- Ask for help or advice.

- Offer to do something for the Controller in the way that they want it done to establish trust.

WHAT TYPE OF COMMUNICATION TOOLS WORK THE BEST FOR A CONTROLLER?

Face-to-Face and Telephone:

Face-to-face and telephone conversations can be effective disarming techniques if you are factual and don't respond with emotions. Recognize a Controller's accomplishments during the discussion. Follow up any meetings with a written (e.g., email) document on the decisions or actions from the conversation. Controllers regard accomplishments more than relationships.

Email and Text:
Email and texting can be effective when working with a Controller if the emails are brief, factual, and to the point. It is not constructive to have extensive email back and forth with a Controller. If there is any discussion, it is better to pick up the phone and call or go see them face-to-face.

Meetings and Presentations:
Meetings and presentations can be challenging when working with a Controller. Controllers can be disruptive in meetings because they can push people's buttons and make them react emotionally. Meetings need to be moderated closely so the Controller doesn't take over or say things that cause negative emotion in the attendees.

Immediately stop any negative statements from a Controller, using a calm and unemotional tone.

If the meeting or presentation topic may cause the Controller to lash out, it is better to meet with the Controller ahead of time to work out any of their concerns.

Written Reports:
Written reports are good for Controllers as long as the report is well written and precise. Request the Controller review the report and provide any comments in written form before the report is finalized.

Let's look at the two scenarios to see what could be done to create a different outcome.

Eve had always tried to handle issues herself before escalating them to her boss, but she perceived Neal was a different case. Eve decided to stop by Neal's office at least twice a day, giving him a status of her activities. Neal did know what he was doing, and when she informed him with short factual statements, it seemed to make him feel more comfortable and relax a little bit. During these short encounters, Eve started telling Neal of any issue that might affect deadlines. Eve never went to Neal without writing up her status in short bulleted points so she could formulate her words before the meeting. Eve noticed that if she started verbally wandering around and didn't get to the point quickly, Neal would cut her off and dismiss what she was trying to say. If Neal ever started becoming sharp and critical, Eve took a deep breath and didn't respond. She just let Neal talk, then went back to the status. Eve always took the time to thank Neal at the end of the meeting. Over the next few weeks, Neal started to trust Eve and allow her some autonomy.

Eve made it a point to give Neal frequent status updates in short, factual statements and to thank him for his expertise and hard work. She also made it a point to detach from his criticisms and realize they were not personal. Disengaging emotionally from Neal allowed her to focus on the facts, helping Neal to trust Eve's abilities.

In Jay's assessment of Sally, he found she was extremely smart, worked hard, and had cleaned up a lot of issues within the organization in a short period of time. Because of her competency, Sally most likely had good reasons to ask for work to be done in a certain way. Sally was feeling like she was pitted against everyone else, which escalated her controlling behavior. Jay stopped by Sally's office twice a day to recognize her dedication to the job. When he agreed with her, he made a point of siding with Sally's opinion in meetings, to build up trust. He thanked her for her expertise and hard work in front of other team members. Jay talked calmly with her individually about creating a positive environment and building trust within her organization. Jay also worked with her to decide what individuals within her department were ready for more responsibility so she could take on special projects and the individuals on her team could grow. Jay worked with Sally to make sure she felt recognized for her hard work and her value within the company.

Jay reduced Sally's stress level, thus reducing her extreme controlling. He worked hard to get Sally's trust and to lessen her sense of being threatened. Jay also worked with Sally to give others more autonomy, reducing Sally's workload and allowing her team to grow. This reduced Sally's stress level and her controlling behavior.

Chapter Summary

Controllers want things done the "right way"—which is their way. Controllers are motivated by power and exercising influence over others. Controllers give unwanted advice, interfere with others, and obsess on the specifics of how things happen.

- Have you worked with someone who takes over groups, tells others what to do and how to do it, does not delegate, and knows what is best for everyone? How does that make you feel? What was the impact this person had on the group?

- What could you have done differently to work with and disarm the Controller?

- Have you ever micromanaged and relished the power and control you had over others?

- What impact do you think this had on the people you were managing? How could you have acted differently to help create more unity?

Make it a point to recognize the Controller's contributions to the workplace and help them reduce their stress levels. Be clear and concise with a Controller, and stay calm.

Chapter 8

The Perfectionist

WHO ARE THEY?

Perfectionists are goal oriented and expect perfection in themselves and others. A Perfectionist will spend a lot of time tweaking their work and others' to make sure it is just right. Perfectionists are driven by their fear of failure and will often conceal mistakes because of fear of judgment from others.

A Perfectionist usually provides too much information and is easily frustrated about perceptions of equity, fairness, and order.

A Controller and Perfectionist can seem similar in their behaviors, but their motivations are very different. A Controller has a need to exert external power over others. Perfectionists have an internal vision of an ideal. Perfectionists set extremely high standards for themselves and others, accompanied by criticism of self and others.

Below are two scenarios. In the first example, a Perfectionist is leading a team and ends up doing most of the work himself. In the second scenario, a leader causes his team to be inwardly focused on giving him perfect status documents, thus disallowing them time or energy to perform the rest of their jobs.

The director of a midsize research center asked William to be the team leader for a research proposal that could potentially bring in a large grant. William organized a meeting with the other team members to figure out a plan. He created a timeline and divvied out responsibilities to get the grant written. Subsequently, William began to feel pressure from his boss to make sure they delivered a stellar proposal; recently, the center's budget had been cut and really needed the income to stay viable. When William began receiving the information from his team members, he became extremely critical of their work and redid some of their sections. Team members soon noticed his rewrites and began to resent William's "I can do this better" attitude. As they continued developing the grant proposal, others' contributions decreased in quality and were often late. William ended up having to write more and more of the grant proposal himself. He delivered the proposal and made his boss happy, but he worked many long days under terrible stress prior to the deadline.

Perfectionists need recognition for their work accomplishments. Their self-worth depends largely on perceiving themselves as perfect. William was chosen to lead the team because he was highly skilled at writing grants and getting things done. Unfortunately, when feeling stressed, his high expectations created tension for himself and his team. As the deadline approached and his stress levels increased, William became overly critical of others' work. To make sure that "it got done right," he started taking on more work than what he could reasonably handle.

David started out as an engineer and worked his way up through the ranks to become vice president of a very large high-tech company. He was known for being a brilliant, thorough engineer whose designs worked the first time. As his career advanced, David became increasingly hard on his teams. He personally worked many, many long days and weekends to make sure everything met his exacting standards. David now had three layers of managers working below him. Despite having received mentoring about delegating more and working at a higher, more strategic level, David continued to micromanage his team. He asked for detailed status reports and often lectured his managers on the "right" way to do the work. Much of his organization's energy was spent providing the detailed information David requested and redoing internal reports and presentations over and over to his precise standards. The organization was spending so much time on inwardly focused activities that the company's customers felt ignored.

David fell into the pattern that overtakes many Perfectionists: micromanagement. Because of his leadership position, he was able to demand and receive the information he wanted from his employees. More than likely, he had legitimate suggestions for people to consider, but the company needed a leader with a vision to move the company forward. When David became so focused on the details of the day-to-day operation, he lost sight of the bigger picture. He may have gotten what we wanted in the short term, but this sort of strategy will eventually hold his company back and sabotage its growth potential.

WHAT PROBLEMS CAN A PERFECTIONIST BRING TO YOUR TEAM?

A Perfectionist will show the following characteristics:

- Rigid about time and schedule changes

- May conceal their mistakes

- Won't take risks because of fear of failure

- Takes on too much work

- Expects perfection of self and others

- Excessively redoes work to get it just right

- Does not delegate well; thinks "I can do it better, faster, and more efficiently"

- Frequently provides too much information

The old song from *Annie, Get Your Gun*, "Anything You Can Do, I Can Do Better," is the Perfectionist's personal anthem. It is difficult to work with Perfectionists, especially when they are stressed, because they don't allow any freedom to make mistakes, which adds unnecessary pressure and often sets the stage for a breakdown in morale.

Having a Perfectionist on your team may seem great at first, because they are willing to take on anything you request and do it very well. But the Perfectionist's participation can be detrimental in the long run because they usually take on more than they can handle. Furthermore, they often alienate others by obsessing over a perfect product.

In the first scenario we see William starting out in a calm, efficient manner. However, when the deadlines started looming and the high financial stakes became clear, William's stress caused his Perfectionist tendencies to manifest and affect the team. Others eventually realized that their work was probably going to be heavily scrutinized, disregarded, or redone all together. A vicious cycle emerged in which

William became hypercritical and his team members became less and less responsive. As the deadline approached, William resented them for not handling their tasks, and they resented William for not valuing the contribution they had made . . . or could have made if their supervisor had been more collaborative and encouraging.

In the second scenario, the same Perfectionist behavior that made David an excellent engineer caused issues as he moved up in the organization. David paralyzed his whole organization by requiring subordinates to continually redo work to his exacting standards. Instead of trusting and empowering his team to develop good solutions and approaches, David limited their creativity and the individual growth potential of team members. Worst of all, his behavior would eventually cripple his company's ability to serve its customers and grow its business.

The disadvantages of working with a Perfectionist include the following:

- Perfectionists fear failure and looking foolish. They may conceal their mistakes.

- Perfectionists do not like to try new things, for fear of making a mistake.

- Perfectionists can present themselves as martyrs because no one appears to be working as much, working as hard, or producing results as high quality as they are.

- Perfectionists can be overly critical of others because of their unrealistically high standards.

- Perfectionists get caught up in details and lose sight of the bigger picture.

- Because they don't know how to pace themselves, Perfectionists risk burning out.

HOW CAN YOU COMMUNICATE EFFECTIVELY WITH PERFECTIONISTS?

Perfectionists favor exchanging ideas and information in a clear, concise way. They typically like facts and figures and don't value emotions. Also, it is important to be mindful of time with them; respect their time and allow them to structure their own schedules as much as possible.

When your subordinate is a Perfectionist, make a special point of recognizing his work achievements and accomplishments. Understand that the Perfectionist has very high standards for everyone but, at the same time, lacks confidence in others' abilities. Perfectionists often produce more work output than others, but even when they do it voluntarily, this can result in them feeling they are being used or unfairly treated. Monitor a Perfectionist's workload to avoid burnout. For these individuals, accomplishments matter more than relationships, so watch team dynamics to make sure Perfectionists do not alienate themselves or foster resentment.

If you work for a Perfectionist boss, be sure to thank them for their help and leadership on any given task. When communicating with a Perfectionist, realize they like structure and regard time as precious; keep communications short, accurate, and to the point. Provide consistent and regular updates on how things are going.

Recognize the efforts of Perfectionist coworkers, and don't forget their need for time control and structure. When working together, communicate with them clearly and concisely. Remember, they may be controlling and overly critical, so do not assume they will delegate responsibility very well.

HOW DO YOU DISARM A PERFECTIONIST?

To keep a Perfectionist working optimally, compliment them on their organizational skills and accomplishments. Keep a Perfectionist focused on the schedule; otherwise they will continuously redo work. Achievement is important to them and they need not only to recognize their own work but also to have others recognize it and express appreciation for it.

Techniques for working with a Perfectionist include the following:

- Send a schedule for when things are due.
- Describe the time constraints and structure.
- Help to set priorities and focus on what is most important.
- Make a point to recognize accomplishments.
- Help establish short-, medium-, and long-term goals, and track progress regularly.
- Monitor task load to minimize risk of burnout.
- Recognize hard work and continued commitment.

WHAT TYPE OF COMMUNICATION TOOLS WORK THE BEST FOR A PERFECTIONIST?

Face-to-Face and Telephone:

Having face-to-face and telephone conversations with a Perfectionist can be effective if you work to make sure they know the expectations of the conversation. Perfectionists tend to overshare and can get caught up in letting you know minute details.

Email and Text:

Email and texting can be very effective when working with a Perfectionist. Email allows a Perfectionist time to respond and to make sure the communication is accurate. A Perfectionist tends to put in a lot of details into emails and texting, sometimes overwhelming the reader. It is important to help a Perfectionist write emails with the Bottom Line Up Front (BLUF) so that readers can digest the information quickly.

Meetings and Presentations:

Meetings and presentations can be challenging when working with a Perfectionist. They want all the details to be discussed or presented and can overwhelm meetings. Make sure the Perfectionist understands the expected outcome of the meeting or presentation.

Perfectionists can be very valuable if a meeting is to make sure all the details tie together.

Written Reports:

Written reports are a very good way to communicate with a Perfectionist as long as the report is well written and precise. Perfectionists tend to be great reviewers and creators of reports, because they pay attention to all the small details.

Let's look at the two scenarios to see what could be done to create better teamwork and disarm the Perfectionist.

When the team members noticed William was becoming overly controlling and critical, they set up short daily meetings to check in and inform him about the work that was getting done. William's comments, for the most part, really did make the grant proposal better, so they made sure they conveyed their appreciation. Instead of getting angry at William's comments, they looked at each comment he sent and provided constructive feedback or a commitment for implementation. For the comments they did not implement, the team gave well-thought-out responses. Because William was very time-oriented, the team worked hard to meet the schedule deadlines, so he felt comfortable placing trust in them.

The team adjusted to William's Perfectionist behavior and figured out a way they all could work together to add value to the proposal. They set up daily meetings to track progress and provide status reports, and they went out of their way to recognize William's hard work and knowledge.

> The team perceived that when David was under stress, he became overly critical and controlling, wanting the job done to his exacting standards. They met with David to explain how much of their time was spent doing internal reporting. They proposed a schedule that included weekly customer communication and meetings, plus twice-daily short verbal meetings with David on project status. This met David's need for detail to assure him that work was progressing well while reducing the amount of time they spent on status reports. In reducing David's stress level, the meetings alleviated the worst of his Perfectionist behavior. By meeting David's needs, the team started to develop trust with him and freed themselves to contribute more effectively to the overall strategic direction of the company.

David's team needed to adjust when his stress level caused him to become critical and controlling. Frequent communication helped David experience trust for his team and spend less time on Perfectionist behaviors, making everyone able to help the organization take care of its customers.

Chapter Summary

Perfectionists are goal oriented and expect perfection in themselves and in others. Perfectionists do not delegate well because they believe they can do it better. Perfectionists are driven by their fear of failure. A Perfectionist usually provides too much information.

- Can you think of a time when you had a Perfectionist in your life and very high, unrealistic standards were set for you? How did it make you feel?

- What do you think you could have done to create a better working environment? How could you have disarmed the Perfectionist?

- Have you ever tweaked the same thing over and over to make it perfect? Do you provide too much detailed information when communicating with people? How do others react to these behaviors?

To work with a Perfectionist effectively, provide a schedule and establish priorities so the Perfectionist knows the time constraints and what to focus on first. Keep track of a Perfectionist's activity levels and help them to delegate and not take on too much work. Recognize a Perfectionist's hard work and commitment.

Chapter 9

The Yes-Man

WHO ARE THEY?

Yes-Men (and of course this term includes women) are always trying to please the people around them and will usually do what is asked (or what they *assume* is asked) without question. They instinctively avoid conflict and become stressed when disharmony occurs. A Yes-Man is motivated primarily to keep the peace, which will not necessarily ensure the organization's success. If a Yes-Man sees something wrong, they may not say anything except to a person they trust deeply.

The greatest danger with Yes-Men is that they provide false encouragement; because of their motivation to please, they may not fully share what they think or feel, even when problems develop. This, in turn, creates misunderstandings and may lead other team members to invest time, energy, and money on efforts founded on inaccurate data.

Below are two scenarios where a Yes-Man's behavior adversely affected an organization. In the first example, a Yes-Man has let down her team, affecting the outcome of an important event. In the second example, a manager sabotages her career and professional reputation because her Yes-Man behaviors keep her from being effective.

Judy agreed to be on the conference-planning committee for the local chapter of her professional association. Before the first meeting, Judy and a few colleagues agreed that last year's conference had been a fiasco, mainly because of its complicated, expensive location. At the first committee meeting, Bob, the chair, assigned Judy to set up the location. At one point the discussion of roles became heated. Judy stayed silent, though she felt uncomfortable with the role she had been given; she thought there was already too much conflict and didn't want to add to it. Next, Bob stated that he wanted the event to be at the same place as last year, because it was a big-name downtown location. Though she knew that others wanted a cheaper, more easily accessed location, Judy said nothing. She didn't want to rock the boat. Others kept looking at her with growing frustration, waiting for her to express her views. Finally, someone barked, "Judy, what do you think?" She stammered and didn't answer the question.

Yes-Men tend to over-adapt because of their need for acceptance and belonging. In the scenario above, Judy did not want any conflict. She did not want to be caught between Bob's wishes and the opinions of the other committee members. Because of her self-doubt, she allowed Bob to sway the decision, even though she and others disagreed with him.

Karen was asked to spearhead the effort to revamp company policies. She brought together members from human resources, training and development, quality assurance, contract, legal, finance, and senior staff to participate in a kickoff meeting. Karen encouraged discussion and listened carefully but said little herself. After the meeting, Karen wanted to include everything that people proposed, but budgetary constraints allowed for implementation of only about 20 percent of the ideas from the meeting. Her boss offered her some ideas on what to include but didn't indicate a preference for any specific approach. At the next meeting, Karen presented a plan, informing the group that she had run these ideas by her boss. She implied that the boss had strong feelings about the plan, and she had gone along with his suggestions. When others pushed back, she repeated her insinuation that the orders had come from above. However, Karen let the team continue to talk; the disharmony in the room made her nervous, but she felt more uncomfortable asserting herself to halt it. When the meeting was adjourned, everyone left in a huff.

Karen disempowered herself by not taking responsibility for decision-making. She used subtle manipulation to avoid becoming the object of criticism. In addition, she created an "us and them" mentality that can create bonding on some levels but usually at the cost of creating harmful dynamics in the overall organization. Karen did herself a huge disservice in the end, because everyone on the team got the non-verbal message that she lacked the power or authority to really effect the change for which she had been made responsible. In the future, when people in Karen's organization want to get something done, they will be more likely to bypass her and go straight to her boss.

WHAT PROBLEMS CAN YES-MEN BRING TO YOUR TEAM?

A Yes-Man shows the following characteristics:

- Can't make decisions
- Needs to please
- Becomes immobilized if disharmony occurs
- Over-adapts to others
- Wishy-washy in decision-making
- Lacks assertiveness
- Experiences self-doubt
- Has trouble saying no
- Sends mixed messages, which can be misconstrued and create extra work for others
- Doesn't ask directly for things
- Invites criticism
- Feels personally rejected

Yes-Men are conflict avoiders. They will keep issues hidden if they think they will cause disharmony, especially if they believe anger or disappointment will be directed at them. Yes-Men will go out of their way to make sure there is peace in the organization. Even though most issues are easier to resolve if found early, Yes-Men will not disclose problems if they believe conflict will ensue.

Let's look at the two scenarios above to see what kind of impact they had on the team.

In the first example, Judy's behavior adversely affected the other committee members. Yes-Men work well when paired with controlling supervisors, but for team dynamics, they can become a liability. By not speaking up with their input, she let the committee down. Judy felt it was more important to not upset the chair than to back up the other members and do what was best for the project. Ironically, even though Judy may have avoided one uncomfortable conversation, she lost the respect of her colleagues and compromised their efforts. The team will most likely see Judy as a good person to carry out directives but not as a real contributor or leader for the overall project.

In the second scenario, Karen squandered an opportunity to demonstrate her leadership and organization skills and gain the respect of her coworkers. She sent a very loud and clear message that she did not have any power or authority in her job position. Chances are she will not be promoted, or if she is, it will most likely be done by a controlling boss who wants to micromanage everything and simply use her as a device for carrying out his directives.

Disadvantages of being or working with Yes-Men include the following:

- They want people to like them, but they sacrifice respect and authority because they can't make the tough decisions.

- Yes-Men risk being seen as ineffective team players because they bail when the going gets tough, leaving the hard decisions up to others.

- Yes-Men tend to miss professional opportunities because they do not like to take risks. They play it safe and rarely make moves to advance their careers.

- Because they have a hard time saying no and do not set reasonable boundaries, Yes-Men can become the dumping ground for duties others dislike.

- Yes-Men do not give honest and necessary feedback if it goes against someone else's strongly stated desires or agenda.

- Yes-Men can't give needed perspective to help a team see the entire picture. Because of their avoidance of conflict, they impair the team's ability to catch problems early.

HOW CAN YOU COMMUNICATE EFFECTIVELY WITH THE YES-MAN?

These individuals must have a trusted, safe place to discuss difficult issues. Yes-Men should not be blamed for bringing up problems. Instead, they need warm conversations and gentle leading up to the point. Yes-Men prefer face-to-face conversations but will respond to email, text, and meetings as long as these are not abrupt or abrasive. Yes-Men tend to be nurturing and easily acknowledge their feelings.

The best method to use in approaching a person who avoids conflict depends a lot on the nature of the relationship. For example, a Yes-Man who is in a supervisory position will often say yes to his own supervisors and then expect his team to support and implement the decision. Many times this leads to unreasonable expectations on which his subordinates must deliver. If your boss is a Yes-Man, it is extremely important to have regular meetings in which you show him or her the work being done, discuss reasonable timelines, and establish prioritization for what he or she would like accomplished. Putting expectations and discussions in writing is a good way to ensure understanding of roles, responsibilities, and outcomes by your Yes-Man.

When you are working with colleagues or subordinates who avoid conflict, reassure them that their perspective is valuable. Remind them that everyone brings a wide array of experiences and skills to an organization. Their perspective is unique and important because it may help to inspire new ways of doing things and contribute to the end product. In other words, do all you can to provide an environment where they feel safe and valued while expressing their opinions and concerns.

If your subordinate is a Yes-Man, encourage him or her to make decisions on their own. If they doubt themselves, be available for them to run ideas past you until they start gaining confidence. Provide support if they receive resistance from others. In addition, to help the Yes-Man grow professionally, make a point to ask for their perspective in meetings, and provide positive reinforcement. This helps the Yes-Man get comfortable with conveying ideas in front of group of people.

When your customer is a Yes-Man, it is especially important to make sure that all expectations are clearly communicated and that they represent accurately what they want. A lot of resources can be wasted if the team and customer are not on the same page. Putting extra effort toward clarity could save unnecessary and expensive remediation.

HOW DO YOU DISARM A YES-MAN?

To motivate a Yes-Man to perform at his best, look to see if he or she is feeling the need to please, is over-adapting, has difficulty making decisions, or seems wishy-washy.

The Yes-Man needs to be around people who like and care for him or her, and to whom he or she can show warmth and caring. Personal relationships matter to them, and they perceive coworkers as extended family.

Environment influences Yes-Men; they will feel and perform best in settings that please or pamper their senses. They prefer a work setting that is warm, friendly, and "homey." They will work best when they feel accepted, wanted, and noticed as an individual.

Techniques for working with a Yes-Man include the following:

- Say, "I'm glad you're here. You're important to the company and to me."
- Help the Yes-Man to feel a personal connection to the team.
- Make sure the Yes-Man has a way to work with others; they will not thrive in solitary activities.
- Spend time talking about the Yes-Man's family.
- Reassure the Yes-Man that his or her perspective is unique and important.
- Provide opportunities for social interactions, both individually and in group settings.
- Have regular face-to-face meetings to discuss work and reassure him or her of their strengths and talents.
- When appropriate, positively reinforce assertiveness and good decision-making.

WHAT TYPE OF COMMUNICATION TOOLS WORK THE BEST FOR A YES-MAN?

Face-to-Face and Telephone:

Having face-to-face and telephone conversations with a Yes-Man is the best way to get the Yes-Man comfortable and relaxed. They want to make sure everything is OK and prefer in-person communication.

Email and Text:

Yes-Men tend to agonize over emails to make sure they are not offensive or harsh. They are also very sensitive to the tone of emails they receive. When sending emails or texts to Yes-Men, make sure the email starts off with pleasantries to get them comfortable and relaxed.

Meetings and Presentations:

Meetings and presentations can work for Yes-Men as long as they are not full of conflict. Conflict drains and stresses a Yes-Man. Meetings that are supportive will allow the Yes-Man to feel comfortable giving their opinions.

Written Reports:

Yes-Men do well when they are asked to either read or write reports.

Let's look at the two scenarios to see what could be done to create a different outcome.

> Before the next meeting, Judy's colleagues realized that she had difficulty giving her opinion in a large meeting if she thought it might be opposed by others. They knew she liked to keep the peace. They decided to show her their support. When Bob reiterated he wanted to hold the meeting in the same place as last year, one of the committee members said, "Judy is very competent to look at different locations and pick the one that best meets our needs. Let's leave it with her." This had the effect of boosting Judy's self-confidence and providing her a safe place to speak up. As a result, she was able, in a nonthreatening way, to start talking about the benefits of other locations. By actively encouraging Judy to share her thoughts, the other members made her more at ease with being a useful contributor.

For Judy, positive and supportive human relationships are vital to her existence on a team. Helping her to know that she is valued and an important member will go a long way to helping her feel comfortable and able to do her best work. Reassuring Judy, publicly and privately, that her unique skills and abilities are necessary to the team will keep her functioning at her optimum level.

Karen's boss recognized that Karen needed support. He asked her to break down the ideas and her conclusions. He then met with Karen and went over her approach and outlined expectations and possible outcomes. Before the next meeting, he asked her to send a reminder email with an agenda. He coached her to start the meeting with a summary of the project, to acknowledge people's contributions, and then ask leading questions of the entire group about the pros and cons of the topics discussed. Because she was prepared, she realized that she had valuable information to offer and felt capable and prepared to state her thoughts. She outlined all the options and why she recommended certain decisions. She showed everyone a well-thought-out set of options and recommended decisions. The team was able to come to decisions for many of the options. After the meeting, her boss met with her in person. He asked her to show the results and got her perspective on the outstanding decisions.

For Karen, self-awareness was important. Her boss helped her recognize her need for moral support. She was then able to seek it out. She also made a point to demonstrate leadership skills and follow basic techniques for running an effective meeting. By being prepared and knowing the art of facilitating discussions, she was able to interject her valuable opinions, seek the feedback of the entire group about what was being suggested by individuals, and also guide the group to make decisions. She not only created buy-in for the project, she was also able to generate enthusiasm.

Chapter Summary

Yes-Men are always trying to please the people around them and will usually do what is asked of them without question. They avoid conflict and become stressed when disharmony occurs. A Yes-Man's overriding concern is to keep the peace and not necessarily to ensure the organization's success.

- Have you ever thought someone was very easy to work with and then you got frustrated because they would not make a decision?
- How could you have helped build up the confidence of this person?
- Do you avoid all conflict and become stressed when any disharmony occurs? Do you not speak up or have difficulty making a decision because it will cause conflict? How can you change that behavior in yourself?

Yes-Men should not be blamed for bringing up problems or be harshly confronted. They need warm conversations, connections with others, and gentle discussions. Yes-Men prefer to have face-to-face conversations and to work in caring teams.

Chapter 10

The Drama Queen

WHO ARE THEY?

There is a Drama Queen on every team—and of course the Drama Queen is not limited to women. The person thrives on attention, spins small issues into disasters, always tops your stories with a tale of their own, and wants to be in the center of attention. Drama Queens can take minor conflicts as personal affronts; will blame others if they screw up; have dramatic mood shifts; dominate any social gathering; and will overshare.

The Drama Queen wants to be in the thick of activities and tends to have self-esteem issues that were never resolved. The Drama Queen thrives on attention because they feel invisible and unimportant. This can lead the Drama Queen to create conflict and then act like a victim.

Drama Queens are trying to convince everyone, including themselves, that they matter.

Drama Queens can be charismatic, funny, and fascinating storytellers. However, they can be very draining because relationships are not balanced. It is all about them.

Below are two scenarios where a Drama Queen's behavior has adversely affected a team. In the first scenario, a Drama Queen caused a team member to retreat, and this stopped the free flow of communication. In the second scenario, a Drama Queen disrupted the team so much that others felt forced to lash out at her negative influence.

Dan sighed. It was time for his Monday morning staff meeting. Meetings used to be productive and sometimes fun. His team had been very close and would do social events together after work. That had all stopped within the last few weeks.

Mike, a recent addition to the team, had begun taking over meetings. He told many stories about the incredible things that happened to him over the weekend. That usually progressed to all the slights he had received, such as Mary leaving him off of an email. She kept trying to tell Mike it was just a mistake, but he would not let it go.

As a result of Mike's antics, Dan started having a hard time maintaining control. A recent meeting ended up with everyone either shutting down or complaining. When Mike first started, he was really fun and his stories were hysterical, even though he was clearly exaggerating. Now that Mike was focusing his drama on the office, it became draining and distracting. Coworkers hid in their cubes with earbuds on instead of talking or socializing. His team's camaraderie and possibly productivity were at risk.

Dan had a big deadline approaching and needed his team to be at their best. He had received complaints from other groups about how disruptive Mike had become. His behavior was wearing down synergistic relationships that had built over time.

Dan let Mike's drama take over team interactions. Mike's stories were fun and exciting when they were directed outside of work. When

Mike started focusing his drama internally to the company, it was very disruptive and caused the team to retreat.

Cindy burst into Xavier's office, weeping that Lin was mean and hated her. Xavier sat Cindy down, gave her some tissues, and asked for the whole story. In between sobs she said, "Lin told me to shut up and go get some work done. I can't work with that kind of anger and meanness!"

Xavier empathized with Cindy and told her he was sure Lin didn't hate her. He spent forty minutes calming her down and said he would speak with Lin. Xavier was worried because this was the third incident between the two. Lin was his best worker, and she was usually very even keel, but she'd complained to Xavier several times about Cindy's talking and drama. He couldn't lose Lin; he needed to do something.

Xavier had ignored Cindy's drama to the point that others were telling her to stop and get to work. They were becoming less productive because of the distractions and feeling frustrated by trying to work in a drama-filled environment. Xavier hoped it would all blow over, but Cindy's over-the-top behavior was escalating, and he was playing into her drama by giving it attention.

WHAT PROBLEMS CAN A DRAMA QUEEN BRING TO YOUR TEAM?

A Drama Queen will show the following characteristics:

- Thrives on attention
- Spins small issues into disasters
- Takes minor conflicts as personal affronts

- Blames others
- Dominates social gatherings
- Overshares and betrays secrets
- Has dramatic mood shifts

Drama Queens can wreak havoc on your organization. They can undermine your authority because your team doesn't want to upset him or her. The Drama Queen wants personal gain in the form of attention and will get it at others' expense.

Let's look at the previous two scenarios to see what kind of impact the Drama Queen had on those around them.

In scenario one, Mike's actions were breaking apart a close-knit group and causing them to retreat and tune out at work. The team's productivity was reduced by their isolation.

In scenario two, Lin, and probably others on the team, had hit their limit and were beginning to push back against Cindy's disruptions.

Disadvantages of working with a Drama Queen include the following:

- Drama Queens spin small issues into large disasters. They cause the team to lose perspective on the relative importance of issues. The negative drama and emotion reduce productivity.

- Drama Queens take personal affront and find scapegoats when they screw up. They are quick to point fingers at others when they make a mistake instead of taking responsibility.

- Drama Queens want to be in the center of attention, and when that slips away from them, they will behave in ways to bring the attention back: dominate social gatherings; betray secrets and gossip; cry or show other dramatic behavior.

HOW CAN YOU COMMUNICATE EFFECTIVELY WITH A DRAMA QUEEN?

Avoid asking a Drama Queen how they are feeling. This usually leads a Drama Queen to complain or to overshare, so minimize personal talk.

Instead, keep the discussion to facts. Drama Queens tend to exaggerate, blow things out of proportion, and editorialize. For example, they might say things like "John hates me," if John is hurrying and doesn't stop to chat. Don't get sucked into the drama. Ask the Drama Queen to summarize what happened in one sentence. That will force them to get to the facts of the issue. Repeat back the facts that you heard, taking out all emotion, empathy, and compassion.

Ask the Drama Queen what they can do about the issue. This pushes the actions back to them. Don't tell them what to do, as this feeds drama. Just listen and ask what actions they can take.

Do not reward negative behavior. Drama Queens will exaggerate their emotions, acting more upset than they actually are. Disengage and don't react.

Finally, understand how you are invested in and encourage the drama. Do you give the Drama Queen attention when there is drama? Do you like the energy, the titillation that comes with the stories? Own up to your part in keeping the drama going.

HOW DO YOU DISARM A DRAMA QUEEN?

Drama Queens thrive on attention and need to know they are not invisible.

Techniques for working with a Drama Queen include the following:

- Be clear on roles and responsibilities and set clear boundaries on expectations.

- Don't respond to the drama but keep the discussions to the facts.
- Provide a way for the Drama Queen to receive positive attention and recognition (for example, an award for work well done, thanking them for work completed on time).
- Don't allow emotions to sneak into discussions.

WHAT TYPE OF COMMUNICATION TOOLS WORK THE BEST FOR A DRAMA QUEEN?

Face-to-Face and Telephone:
Drama Queens thrive on face-to-face conversations. When you meet with a Drama Queen, make sure you do not get caught up in feelings of intrigue and excitement. Stay focused on the facts and be precise in your speech.

Email and Text:
Email and texting can be effective when working with a Drama Queen as long as the emails are factual, without any controversy or emotional ambiguity. If emails or texts start having emotional content, stop the email chain and go talk to the Drama Queen in person.

Meetings and Presentations:
Meetings and presentations can be difficult with a Drama Queen. They have an audience and sometimes will exaggerate for effect. To keep the Drama Queen controlled, it is important to have an agenda, stick to it, and prevent a lot of extraneous talking.

Written Reports:
Written reports are good for Drama Queens, because reports are typically precise and concise without avenues to create drama.

Let's look at the two scenarios to see what could be done to alleviate the drama.

> Dan realized that Mike's over-the-top behavior was disrupting his team. Dan called Mike into his office. First, he said that Mike was doing a good job recruiting new personnel and thanked him for his great work. Dan then said matter-of-factly, "Mike we have a large agenda for the next meeting. I need to start on time and get right to business because it's crunch time. I need you to help me keep things focused and on task and to give all your energy to making the deadline for your assignment." Mike felt important and was getting the attention he wanted. At the meeting, Dan came in and immediately presented an agenda with a timeline for each topic. When the discussion started to go off track, Dan brought it back to the agenda. The team was more engaged than Dan had seen them in a long time. Mike's drama was reduced while he focused on the resources the company needed to meet the deadline. Dan stopped by twice a day to thank Mike for all his hard work.

Dan let Mike know (in a roundabout way) that he needed Mike's disruptions in the staff meetings to stop. He stated the importance of a structured format and did it in a way that made Mike feel important. As a result, Mike didn't feel a need to create drama in order to gain attention from Dan and the team.

> Xavier had let the situation between Lin and Cindy go on too long. He first checked in with Lin. He hadn't talked to her in a while even though she was his best employee. "I'm totally overwhelmed," she said. "My son is sick and I'm frazzled." Xavier told Lin he would reassign some of her

tasks so she could spend more time at home. Lin looked relieved. Next, Xavier took Cindy out to lunch. He told her how much he appreciated all that she did. Then he said, "You've got an important deadline coming up, though, and I notice you've spent a lot of time socializing lately. You're a good employee, and I want to help you get along in your career."

Cindy took offense. She whined, "Everyone socializes a lot! Why do they complain about me? They're all out to get me, and it makes this a terrible place to work!"

Without raising his voice, Xavier asked if she had evidence of others' behavior. He had her break down her workday in her own words, including when she socialized and when she worked. Xavier then asked Cindy what she could do about being more productive. Whenever Cindy started exaggerating or bringing in emotions to the conversation, Xavier brought it back to just the facts. At the end of the lunch, Xavier had an agreement from Cindy to curb her socialization and drama in order to meet her deadlines.

Xavier gave Cindy positive attention for a job well done but also told her she needed to reduce her socializing. Cindy liked the attention that a lunch with the boss gave her. She was ecstatic that Xavier wanted to help her career. When Cindy started to escalate drama, Xavier kept to the facts, didn't respond to the emotions, and had Cindy work toward a solution.

Chapter Summary

The Drama Queen thrives on attention, takes small issues and makes them disasters, tops others' stories with their own, and overshares. Drama Queens can take minor conflicts as personal affronts, can have dramatic mood shifts, and act like victims. The Drama Queen wants to be in the middle of activities. Drama Queens tend to exaggerate and blow things out of proportion.

- What impact does a Drama Queen have on your workplace?

- What can you do immediately to defuse this behavior? How can you disarm the Drama Queen?

- Have you ever spun small issues into larger disasters to be in the middle of the attention? Do you feel compelled to top others' stories with ones of your own? Can you see the impact this behavior has on the people around you? What can you do to change this behavior?

Don't get sucked into the drama. Ask the Drama Queen to summarize what happened in one sentence. That will force them to get to the facts of the issue. Repeat back the facts you heard, taking out all emotion, empathy, and compassion. Ask the Drama Queen what they can do about an issue. This pushes the actions back to them. Do not engage in the drama. Just listen, and ask what actions they can take.

Chapter 11

The Recluse

WHO ARE THEY?

Recluses are reflective and imaginative and are often the creative engine of many revolutionary ideas. However, they typically do not do well implementing their ideas. They often become overwhelmed and have difficulty prioritizing multiple assignments.

Recluses need time alone to think and process. Instead of being motivated by schedules and time constraints, Recluses tune out. They withdraw when there are too many people around or there is too much pressure.

Below are two scenarios where Recluses' behavior adversely affects the people around them. In the first example, a Recluse is the boss of a program, and his withdrawal has frustrated his subordinates. In the second scenario, the Recluse is a vendor who missed many deadlines, negatively impacting the project's deliverables.

Jay had gone by his boss's office three times today, but the door always seemed to be shut. Jay had sent an email and left two phone messages, but

Carl was just not getting back to him. Jay had a serious problem with his project, and Carl needed to know about it. Jay sighed. The whole office was very frustrated with Carl's lack of engagement. At lunch with another program manager yesterday, they had spent the whole time talking about how hard it was to have Carl as a boss. Jay liked Carl because he had an interesting perspective on problems, had amazing creative ideas, was hands-off, and never tried to micromanage. But lately Carl, when he actually went to a meeting, was disengaged and in his own world. Jay was so frustrated that he pounded on the office door.

Carl's team liked his perspective and his ideas for advancing projects. However, Carl didn't like the day-to-day aspects of people and business management. He found it very difficult and plodding to do all the detailed financial analysis required in his job. He liked Jay in particular, because Jay was proactive, would do all the detail work, and make decisions without bothering him. Carl did not feel any pressure when his email was building up; he figured if it was something important, someone would come by his office. Unfortunately, Carl's withdrawal was threatening to sabotage the project and perhaps jeopardize the continued services of one of his favorite employees.

Melanie, an engineer and team leader on a large construction project, was waiting for some design modifications from Tim, the architect. Tim was a genius . . . but eccentric. He disliked attending meetings and would go for days without checking his email. His designs were revolutionary, but some building code corrections remained to be completed. The updates she had received lacked documentation or instructions. Construction could not begin until this was done. Melanie had never been so angry or frustrated with someone in her whole life! She had deadlines to meet and impatient construction vendors who were expecting completed blueprints. She had to put in extra hours to figure out if the correct changes had even been made. The project was fast approaching the deadline, and Melanie needed those final updates. She was forced to drive two hours to his office to talk with him in person and impress upon him the importance of the deadline.

Recluses respond favorably to interesting ideas and love reflecting on difficult problems. Thus, Tim was more motivated by the next new project than by correcting the blueprints he had already created. Tim hated changing his drawings to satisfy government building codes; he much preferred to move on to the next interesting idea. Tim did not bother looking at his email or picking up his phone, because he found both activities annoying, and besides, they interrupted his thoughts.

WHAT PROBLEMS CAN A RECLUSE BRING TO YOUR TEAM?

A Recluse shows the following characteristics:

- Tunes out of the discussion or situation
- Starts tasks and doesn't finish them
- Has difficulty prioritizing multiple assignments
- Does not volunteer
- Daydreams
- Is overly slow to get out materials
- Is nonresponsive

Recluses withdraw when there is too much pressure or so many multiple assignments that they cannot prioritize. They retreat even more when there is time or schedule pressure. Recluses have great ideas but have difficultly following through and completing tasks.

Let's look at the two scenarios described earlier to see what kind of impact the Recluses had on the organization.

In scenario one, Carl wanted his team to take on the responsibility and authority for the project and make the needed decisions. He withdrew and was not responsive. This made his team, especially Jay, frustrated and angry. Jay didn't know how to get Carl to be more engaged, and the team was losing respect for their boss, thanks to his disengagement.

In scenario two, Melanie didn't understand how Tim could just ignore the project and their need for required changes. After all, Melanie was paying Tim's company for the product. Tim, on the other hand, just wanted to design the next new buildings and not be bothered with all the details of the actual construction.

Disadvantages of being or working with a Recluse include the following:

- Recluses have difficulty completing tasks. This can hold up a team unless they are given very specific directions and guidance.

- They may be resented by those with whom they work because they check out mentally after the creative work is completed and aren't really there to take ownership of a situation. Team members may feel abandoned.

HOW CAN YOU COMMUNICATE EFFECTIVELY WITH A RECLUSE?

Recluses typically withdraw when communication involves anger, threats, or attacks. When talking to a Recluse, the conversation should be nonthreatening in order to permit the Recluse to reflect and think.

When your boss or customer is a Recluse, know in advance that they are unlikely to complete detailed administrative tasks. Recluses do not mind at all if other people do all the administrative tasks and make decisions. Having a Recluse as a boss will necessitate negotiating authority to permit you to make decisions and support the day-to-day.

If you work with a Recluse, recognize his need to be alone and to think about solutions. Recluses typically are very creative and have lots of good ideas. Recluses need to be told schedules and deadlines before delays create a critical, stress-filled situation. They will not automatically figure out their own agendas. Recluses need to be managed closely if there is any time constraint, because they can get distracted by their own thoughts instead of meeting the deadline.

HOW DO YOU DISARM A RECLUSE?

To disarm a Recluse, give time for solitude and thinking. As much as possible, keep a Recluse focused on a single goal. Remember that the Recluse functions better when undisturbed by people, noises, or outside demands. Give the Recluse a schedule to follow.

Techniques for working with a Recluse include the following:

- Tell the Recluse exactly what is expected, and leave them alone to do it.

- Provide the Recluse with private space.

- Be as direct, comprehensive, and precise as possible.

- Encourage the Recluse to schedule some time alone several times a day.

WHAT TYPE OF COMMUNICATION TOOLS WORK THE BEST FOR A RECLUSE?

Face-to-Face and Telephone:

Face-to-face and telephone calls are the best way to communicate with a Recluse. They are typically not time and schedule oriented and do not feel internal pressure to attend meetings or to read emails or texts.

Email and Text:

Recluses can easily ignore email and texting, so they are not the preferred method of communication.

Meetings and Presentations:

Meetings and presentations can be challenging when working with a Recluse simply because they typically don't like attending. They get lost in thought if the subject is not engaging to them.

Recluses can be very valuable in brainstorming meetings or meetings that need creative and innovative thinking.

Written Reports:

Written reports can be good or challenging for Recluses, depending on the topic. A dry, detailed report that a Perfectionist would love would be hard for a Recluse to create or read. Written reports that have creative content and new ideas work very well for a Recluse to create and read.

Let's look at the two scenarios above to see what could be done to help use the Recluses' strengths.

After having a Perfectionist as his last boss, Jay enjoyed having a lot of responsibility and authority without any micromanagement. He knew Carl did not like administrative details, so he tried to make as many decisions as he could without bothering Carl. Still, Jay realized he needed to do something about this unresponsive behavior or the team's frustration would continue to grow. He wanted to keep Carl as his boss, so he was motivated to find a solution. Jay knew that Carl got in about 9:00 a.m. He decided to try to catch Carl every morning for fifteen minutes. He would drop in with Carl's favorite coffee from the local chain. While Carl drank his coffee, Jay would describe any pressing issues or special successes. Jay also enjoyed the opportunity to get excellent advice from a thoughtful, deep thinker.

Jay realized he really did want Carl to continue as his boss, as he liked working for a Recluse much better than a Perfectionist. Carl had amazing, innovative ideas and really did help the project. The fifteen-minute meeting worked for both of them and each became better at his job.

Melanie could see where a long-term relationship with Tim and his firm could be very profitable to her company; they were well known for innovation and trend-setting design. However, Melanie had to figure out how to get the relationship with Tim structured in a way that worked for both of them.

When she drove to his office, Melanie found Tim wandering around his building, lost in deep thought. Melanie approached him gently so he would not be startled and said, "Good to see you, Tim. Listen, we need corrections to some blueprints in order for construction to begin. Would you mind if one of your associates handles it so you can focus on your new project?" Tim's eyes lit up and he agreed immediately.

Melanie then approached Tim's boss to obtain permission for the associate to begin work on the modifications. Melanie was more than prepared to pay a bonus to the firm if the project was completed on time.

Melanie was excited that she had thought of a way to get the project completed on time while keeping Tim and his company happy. Melanie realized she wanted to bring Tim in on some other projects to get his ideas; after getting an accurate view of Tim's abilities, Melanie believed she understood how to use his strengths and how to relieve Tim of tasks that would bring his weaknesses into play.

Chapter Summary

Recluses are typically reflective and imaginative and are often the creative engine of many revolutionary ideas. However, they typically do not do well implementing their ideas or completing tasks. They have difficulty prioritizing, become overwhelmed, and shut down. Recluses need time alone to think and process. They are not motivated by schedules and time constraints and will withdraw when stressed. Recluses do not feel pressure if their email or voicemail is piling up.

- Do you have someone on your team who gets stressed when there is too much activity and noise?
- What can you do to help that person get alone time but also be part of the team?
- Do you need a lot of alone time to think and process the day? Do you routinely ignore your email because it is not important to you? How do you think these behaviors have affected the teams you work with?

Recluses can be powerful assets to your organization, but they need a private space to think and process. The Recluse needs to be focused on one goal with clear and precise directions.

Chapter 12

The Whiner

WHO ARE THEY?

Whiners are all too easy to find: they're the people who moan, complain, grumble, and blame others for all their difficulties.

It takes emotional energy to fend off complaining at work. People around a Whiner often find their productivity sapped. According to Robert Sapolsky, a professor of neurology and neurological sciences at Stanford University, "Exposure to nonstop negativity can disrupt learning, memory, attention, and judgment."[1]

Whiners can drag down an organization because the negativity can be "catching," and soon your whole organization is thinking about what is wrong instead of what is going right.

Below are two scenarios where a Whiner's behavior has adversely affected a team. In the first example, a Whiner complained about his work. In the second scenario, a Whiner was causing dissension in the organization.

Jim always dreaded going into Bill's office. He had emailed Bill requesting data but had gotten no response. Jim always felt drained after talking to Bill because he habitually blamed other people for his work not getting done and found fault with the company, department, and people.

As soon as Jim sat down, Bill started complaining. "Why do we really need it? It's such a stupid task, and I bet no one even looked at this monthly status report." He then launched into complaining about Laura, a senior analyst. He said she was hard to work with, tried to control every situation, and ignored all of his requests.

Next Bill moved on to discuss management of the company's 401K and how he felt the policies on taking personal time off were antiquated. Jim mumbled that he needed the status no later than tomorrow morning at 8:30 a.m. and left Bill's office as fast as he could.

Jim felt overwhelmed; it seemed Bill wasn't happy with anything or anyone. Jim left every conversation he had with Bill feeling annoyed and exhausted, and he wasn't the only one. Bill's whining wasn't only affecting his own productivity but that of everyone in the department.

Gene, the company quality assurance manager, had just hit his limit working with Tanya, one of the project managers. Tanya was a forceful personality and would come into meetings full of complaints, then just leave saying she had work to do. She was a master at blaming other people for errors or shortfalls in work she should be doing. Tanya routinely blew him off or responded to his emails and requests with curt, flippant replies. Gene had identified a serious quality issue occurring with the product development, but Tanya just rolled her eyes when he brought up the subject. "Relax," she said. "You're just a bean counter, anyway." Gene knew the final product testing was in three weeks, and if things didn't change, he would have to fail the product test. He also knew Tanya would blame the missed deadline on him and the team when she talked to the customer or upper management. Gene knew he needed to do something immediately to fix the situation.

Gene felt as if Tanya didn't take him seriously and just complained, whined, and blamed others for any of her work that wasn't getting done.

WHAT PROBLEMS CAN A WHINER BRING TO YOUR TEAM?

A Whiner will show the following characteristics:

- Whines, complains, grumbles
- Blames problems on others
- Knows which buttons to push and pushes them
- Always points out the negative

Whining and blaming others makes these people feel empowered without taking any real responsibility. Team members dislike feeling dragged down and may not want to work with a Whiner, damaging efficiency. A Whiner can also sabotage your authority. It is easy for whining behavior to be "catching"; before you know it, your whole team may start complaining and blaming others.

You don't want to be seen as someone who condones the whining and complaining, so ignoring a Whiner is not a good solution. You need to help them change the habit.

Let's look at the above two scenarios to see what kind of impact the Whiner had on those around them.

In scenario one, Bill may have had valid points, but his whining was draining, and he was exhausting to be around.

In scenario two, Tanya set up an adversarial relationship, causing emotional turmoil and loss of productivity.

Disadvantages of being or working with a Whiner include the following:

- Whiners place blame on other colleagues, situations, or things, causing dissension among the team.

- The negativity of a Whiner reduces productivity and morale.

- Complaining is catching, and soon a whole team may be whining and grumbling.

HOW CAN YOU COMMUNICATE EFFECTIVELY WITH WHINERS?

Ask the Whiner what they are going to do about a situation. Don't let them get away with just complaining and dodging responsibility for a solution.

To defuse whining, have interaction that is energetic, enthusiastic, upbeat, and lively. When the Whiner starts up, change the subject immediately and ask what good happened this week. Try to help the Whiner change the habit of always looking at negative aspects of a situation.

Many times, a Whiner will blame others for their work not being completed. They need to be given specific responsibility with clear boundaries.

If a Whiner is your boss or customer, be upbeat and friendly. When at all possible, meet with him or her in person. It is better not to respond negatively. Instead, do your best to respond in a clear and friendly manner.

If a Whiner is your team member or a member of a support

organization, do not allow complaints to go unchecked, because he or she will start creating dissension within your team and company. Take the Whiner aside, and in a positive, upbeat, friendly manner, listen to his concerns. Above all, do not isolate a Whiner—it will cause the bad behavior to escalate.

In a meeting, if a Whiner starts complaining, redirect the conversation. Move to the next subject, interrupt in a friendly, upbeat manner by stating some positive things, or disarm them by saying something like, "Wow—you always look at the dark side of things, don't you?" in a playful and light tone.

Sometimes complaints are valid, so don't dismiss the underlying issue. Something in your organization may truly need to be fixed.

HOW DO YOU DISARM A WHINER?

When talking to the Whiner, ask them to help you develop a solution. Sometimes Whiners can point out real issues in an organization. Empower them to create change and to be invested in the changes. If they are part of the solution, their whining will diminish.

Keep the conversation positive and lively if at all possible. Many times, Whiners don't see how their behavior impacts the organization.

Techniques for working with a Whiner include the following:

- Be upbeat and friendly.
- Point out all the good things in the organization.
- Ask them to help develop a solution to the problem.
- When they complain, ask them what is positive—help them to change their habit.

WHAT TYPE OF COMMUNICATION TOOLS WORK THE BEST FOR A WHINER?

Face-to-Face and Telephone:

Whiners thrive on face-to-face conversations. They want an audience. When you meet with a Whiner, make sure you keep the discussion upbeat and lively. If complaining starts, stop them immediately with a new subject or interject with a positive statement. If the Whiner's complaint has merit, ask them what they can do about it.

Email and Text:

Email and texting can be effective when working with a Whiner because it does not give them an audience. Make sure emails are factual and clear. If content becomes emotional and negative, stop the email chain and go talk to the Whiner in person.

Meetings and Presentations:

Meetings and presentations can be difficult with a Whiner. They have an audience and sometimes bring up issues that are off topic. To keep the Whiner controlled, it is important to have an agenda and keep to it. If the Whiner starts up, offer to talk with them outside of the meeting to discuss their issue.

Written Reports:

Written reports are good ways to communicate with Whiners because reports are typically precise and concise without opening up an avenue to complain or whine.

Let's look at the two earlier scenarios to see how the Whiner can be disarmed by listening to their concerns and working with them in a positive way.

Jim made a decision to engage Bill proactively instead of just letting him whine unchecked. The next day, Jim went to Bill and said, "I understand your frustration about the reports. I'll ask who's reading it; maybe it isn't necessary anymore." He then asked Bill some light-hearted questions about his department and gathered the status information he needed verbally. Bill responded to Jim's requests because he felt as if he had been heard. While Jim felt that he hadn't completely stopped the whining, he had made a good start in working with Bill in a positive way.

Jim made the decision to change his own attitude and behavior toward Bill. Once he started thinking about what Bill said, he thought the complaint had merit. Maybe it wasn't being read or it could be changed to be more in line with what was needed. Jim also worked to get the status from Bill verbally instead of requiring a formally written status. That helped Bill to realize Jim was on his side and not someone to attack or ignore.

Gene spent time thinking about how he could work in a productive way with Tanya. He recognized that she had a gift for pulling people together. He decided to approach the next team meeting with a completely different attitude. He looked at all the quality metrics he presented each week and realized that his report focused solely on what was wrong with the product development. Gene flipped all of his charts around to show the metrics in a positive light and was surprised to see incredible progress over a short period of time. He realized he had been so focused on the small number of negative product issues that he had not seen all the successes. Gene went into the next team meeting and presented the positive metrics, praising the team for their hard work and innovation. Gene had printed out the report in bright, cheery colors instead of the black and white he usually used. He saw an instant change in the team's attitude, and for the first time, he saw the depth of their commitment. Tanya liked the positive energy Gene brought to the room, and she not only focused intently on his presentation but also thanked Gene profusely after the meeting.

Gene's changed presentation brought about a focus on success rather than failure. He was able to defuse Tanya's whining and blaming by showing all the team's work in a positive, energetic light—and still presented the necessary metrics to guide the team's future efforts.

Chapter Summary

Whiners complain, grumble, and blame others for all their difficulties. They can harm your organization by shifting focus to the negative instead of the positive.

- How do the Whiners in your life make you feel? How do they impact you and your team?

- How can you disarm people on your team who constantly complain and blame others?

- Have you caught yourself whining and complaining? How do you think that makes others around you feel?

Sometimes Whiners point out real issues. Empower them to help fix the issues so they are part of the solution. Keep conversations with Whiners positive and lively.

Chapter 13

The Liar

WHO ARE THEY?

Liars do not tell the truth in situations. Either they lack courage to be frank or have an expectation of personal gain from deceit. People lie for a variety of reasons: to build up their own image, to cover up an action, to spare others' feelings, to manipulate others, to put others down, to be more likable, to prevent a conflict or negative reaction to a situation, to justify a behavior, to appear more competent, or to avoid consequences of their actions.

Everyone lies! Most of us have told a "white lie" or two—untruths we believe are harmless and allow us to be kind to another person or to avoid conflict. For example, lying that you think your boss's children are absolutely beautiful, or that you are OK with a colleague's choice of restaurant because you know it is his favorite place, or telling your coworker the cookies she brought in were the best you ever had. There is research showing a little bit of lying actually strengthens relationships when you are doing it to help someone or protect their feelings.

This chapter, on the other hand, deals with chronic Liars who do harm to others around them.

Let's look at two scenarios where a Liar's behavior is detrimental to individuals and to the organization. In the first scenario, a Liar is a boss who promises things she has no intention of delivering. The second scenario describes someone who uses likeability and trust to harass a coworker.

Yuan took a deep breath, mustered up his courage, and opened the door to his boss's office. He sat down in the chair and gave Catherine a list of reasons why he deserved a raise: he was a hard worker, always came to work on time, didn't complain about the shifts he received, had multiple customer letters in his file about how helpful he was, and had been at the store for over two years at the same pay rate. Catherine smiled and said yes, he was a great employee, and she would get him a 3 percent increase. Yuan walked out of her office feeling happy.

One month later Yuan had not received the raise, so he followed up with Catherine. She said she was working on it and asked him to be patient. He waited. Another month passed and still no raise. He went back to Catherine—when would he receive the 3 percent increase? Again, Catherine said she was working on it, that things like raises take time for processing.

Yuan pulled aside a coworker from another division and asked if she had ever received a raise. The coworker said yes, every year. She also said it was well known that Catherine lied about everything: about working to rotate the shifts, about fixing the microwave in the employee break room, and about anything that would make work more enjoyable and meaningful to the staff. The coworker told Yuan that Catherine had no intention of giving him a raise and he should not believe her. He asked if anyone

---

had tried to do something about the lies, but the coworker just shrugged and said, "No. They don't want to get fired, so they just transfer out of her division as quickly as possible." Consequently, Yuan went to the HR department and requested a transfer. He made sure all of the commendation letters were in his file.

In the scenario above, Catherine lied to avoid conflict and to avoid increasing cost in the division. She would have to champion employees to the store owner to get raises, and she didn't want to stick her neck out for any employee. Catherine thought only of herself and lacked compassion and empathy. She also lied about being willing to rotate employee shifts because that would take more of her time.

Lindsey had a stress-related stomachache. She couldn't quit work because she was barely paying her bills as it was. She had racked up debt while unemployed. When Lindsey started this job, Louis came over to her desk every morning and made comments about her appearance. He would stand over her while she was seated and look down her shirt. Lindsey started wearing more conservative styles to deter him. Unfortunately, the more modestly she dressed, the lewder his comments became. Now Louis was usually waiting at her cube when she arrived. As she was taking her coat off and starting to sit down, he routinely groped her bottom. Lindsey had the early shift, so there were very few people in the office and no one around her. She had gone to the company owner to report the problem. A week later, he told her, "I talked to Louis. He assures me he would never intentionally make someone uncomfortable. He's a great guy and everyone likes him. He goes out of his way to help people out, and everyone trusts him. Are you sure you aren't being too sensitive?" Louis laughed at Lindsey the next morning, telling her no one would believe her over him.

In the scenario above, Louis used his reputation to harass another employee, lie to the owner, and continue his bad behavior. Louis obviously has had a lot of experience lying to people and has become quite convincing.

Before looking at how Yuan and Lindsey could handle the situations, let's look at why Liars act the way they do.

WHAT PROBLEMS CAN LIARS BRING TO YOUR PROJECT?

A Liar shows the following behaviors:

- Liars do not tell the truth in order to get some gain.
- Liars are looking out for themselves and not for the team or organization.
- Most chronic Liars seem trustworthy and are convincing and believable.
- Liars typically are quick thinking and have a good memory.

Compulsive lying harms the organization because one person is not working as part of the team, actively damages team unity, and manipulates others. One other aspect of having a compulsive Liar in your organization is the increased chance of fraud. A typical business loses about 5 percent of its revenue due to fraud each year. Someone who routinely deceives others will also commit fraud more easily.

Some people continuously lie because of the imagined consequences of mistakes they make. People are more likely to lie if they are stressed or believe there are negative consequences for telling the truth.

In the first scenario, no one wanted to confront Catherine; it was easier to request a transfer into another division as soon as possible. This caused high attrition and lower productivity (because of the constant churn of new employees) within the division. It also harmed employees who didn't get the financial reward of doing a good job.

In the second scenario, Louis was charming, well liked, and seemed trustworthy when he wasn't. Thanks to Louis's skill as a Liar, the owner didn't take Lindsey seriously, and she felt she had no choice but to put up with unacceptable behavior.

Disadvantages of being or working with a Liar including the following:

- Liars can seem trustworthy and caring, and they are easily believed. This causes team members to question themselves and feel betrayed, frustrated, or angry.

- Liars look out for themselves and are not team players. They cause upheaval and chaos in the organization.

- Liars seed distrust because lies can make people not trust what they hear from anyone.

- Liars are typically confident, quick thinking, and smart because it takes a lot of skill to maintain lies. Their untruths slowly eat away at team trust and confidence.

- Liars can also be intimidating and bullying, particularly if they are in a position of power.

HOW CAN YOU COMMUNICATE EFFECTIVELY WITH A LIAR?

Develop skepticism around people, especially if you have heard repeated complaints. Remember the most accomplished Liars are charming, competent, and seem trustworthy. Be careful jumping to conclusions as to who is telling the truth.

Ask questions to expose inconsistencies. For example, ask for the details about a situation: ask when the action will happen, ask how they found out the information, ask who they spoke with, and so on. The more details you get, the easier it will be to expose a lie.

Act quickly when you notice a lie. Exposing a Liar quickly is very important before damage is done to the organization or team.

If you are concerned that someone is lying to you, document or have a witness to any conversation. A follow-up email is a good technique to let the Liar know you are tracking what they say.

Before any action, try to understand what the person gets out of lying and what their motive might be. You may be able to solve the underlying cause:

- Is the person building up their own image and trying to look better than others?

- Are they covering up an action or inaction that they feel, if exposed will cause them harm?

- Are they justifying something they did by lying about the benefits?

- Are they lying to appear more competent because they are afraid of the consequences of failing?

- Is the lie to reduce negative consequences of their actions?

Don't attack a Liar; it does not solve the issue and may go into finger-pointing and anger. Focus on the problem instead. It is much better to deal with a Liar in person one-on-one than with any other communication method. Attacking or calling out a Liar in a group will escalate the situation. It will also pit you against the Liar—and remember, Liars have a lot of practice manipulating the truth.

When a Liar is your boss or customer, be very careful. Document all of your face-to-face or telephone conversations, and have witnesses to conversations. Ask questions and probe for the details.

Pay attention to body language that doesn't match the words.[1]

HOW DO YOU DISARM A LIAR?

To disarm a Liar, pay close attention to the details of what they are saying. State back to them their lie so they know you are paying attention. Follow up with an email documenting every detail of the conversation.

Try to understand what is motivating the Liar so you can work on solving the underlying problem.

Techniques for working with a Liar include the following:

- Be careful, as practiced Liars are believable and typically seem trustworthy. Don't assume that just because you know and trust someone, they are telling the truth.

- Maintain steady, full eye contact at all times. This will often create a level of nervousness if the person is lying.

- Document all conversations so inconsistencies can be exposed.

- Pay attention to body language that doesn't match the words being stated in order to know what part of the conversation is a lie.

- Try to solve the underlying issue that may be causing the Liar to not tell the truth.

WHAT TYPE OF COMMUNICATION TOOLS WORK THE BEST FOR A LIAR?

Face-to-Face and Telephone:

When you meet with a Liar, document your conversation and send it to the Liar in a written form (e.g., email) so that both of you have a record of the conversation. If you notice a lie during your conversation, ask for details and keep probing. This will make it easier to expose the lie.

Email and Text:

Email and texting can be effective when working with a Liar because the conversations are documented in writing. Liars depend on charm or bullying, so having a written record of conversations is important.

Meetings and Presentations:

Meetings and presentations are effective when working with a Liar. Having a group of people makes it more difficult for the Liar to keep up the façade.

Written Reports:

Written reports are also good for a Liar, because reports are typically more fact-based information that will help to keep the Liar focused on the specific information required for the report.

Let's see how Yuan and Lindsey can be more effective in handling Liars.

Yuan liked the division he was in and wanted to give Catherine one last chance. After his talk with his coworker, Yuan decided to write up each of his conversations with Catherine. He then asked to see her again. This time, he had a coworker (from another division) come along. He caught Catherine in the hallway instead of going into her office. He chitchatted for a moment, asking if she was having a good day and engaging with her. Yuan then said, "I'm really looking forward to the raise you promised!" He thanked her again for putting him in for a raise and told her how much it meant to him. Yuan ended the conversation by asking lightly, "When do you think I might see the increase in my paycheck?" Catherine looked uncomfortable with a witness standing by but said it would come through in his next paycheck. Yuan then sent Catherine an email documenting the agreement. He wrote up the conversation and had the coworker witness the statement. He was then armed with all the information he needed to meet with human resources if Catherine didn't give him the raise.

Yuan disarmed Catherine by engaging with her and making a connection. He also brought a witness to corroborate Catherine's statements. If his raise didn't come through, he would have documentation on what he was promised. He also protected himself by putting in for a transfer for a position that would pay him a higher wage, if the pay increase did not happen.

> Lindsey knew she had to do something dramatic. Since her talk with the owner, Louis's behavior had escalated, as if he relished the fact that Lindsey was not believed. She realized she needed someone else to witness the behavior. First, she wrote up every encounter with Louis with every date and exacting detail. Then Lindsey went to an older woman who worked on the same floor and came in at the same time as Lindsey each day. She took Janet into her confidence and asked for help. Janet was shocked by what she heard because she liked Louis (just like everyone else). She was skeptical but agreed to help. The next morning, before going to her cubical, Lindsey stopped at Janet's office. She then headed to her workspace. Like clockwork, Louis was there grinning at her. Janet approached from the hallway behind Louis and watched as he made a lewd comment and groped Lindsey while her hands were busy with her coat. The older woman gasped and walked directly to the owner's office.

Lindsey found a trusted person to witness Louis's behavior so he would be caught in his lies. She was able to go to the owner with both a witness and the detailed documentation of his actions.

Chapter Summary

Liars either do not have the courage to tell the truth in a group situation or choose to lie for personal gain. People lie for a variety of reasons: to build up their own image, to cover up an action, to spare others' feelings, to manipulate, to put others down, to be more likable, to prevent a conflict or negative reaction to a situation, to justify a behavior, to appear more competent, or to avoid consequences of their actions.

- How does a Liar make you feel? What can you do immediately to help reduce the Liar's impact on you?
- What specific actions can you do to disarm the Liar?
- Have you ever told an untruth and seen the impact of that lie on others? How can you break the habit of lying to others?

Practiced Liars are believable and typically seem trustworthy. Don't assume that because you know and trust someone that they are telling the truth. Pay attention to body language that doesn't match the words being stated. Act quickly when you notice a lie. Document all conversations so inconsistencies will come to light. Exposing a Liar quickly is very important before damage is done to the organization.

Your Own Communication and Leadership Style

Part III provides you with insight into knowing yourself and your management style, techniques to communicate effectively with others, and the five traits of successful leaders.

Effective managers must understand themselves, know what motivates the people around them, and be able to communicate effectively. Your personality type affects your management style. There are four basic management styles: Autocratic, Laissez-Faire, Democratic, and Paternalistic. The most effective manager can change their leadership style, depending upon the team and situation. We explore each management style, how each management style can be the most effective, and how situations can be mismanaged.

One of the most important skills a manager must have is to be able to confront people constructively. One of the primary issues in communication is a misuse of confrontation: it is either completely avoided;

attempted through indirect, back-channel means; or performed in a harsh and negative manner. This part explores confrontation and how to have successful, productive discussions.

Finally, successful leaders exhibit the following five traits: they know themselves; they are able to establish vision and direction; they empower their teams; they align people in positions to maximize each individual strength; and they consistently motivate and inspire. This section looks at each of these attributes, especially as they apply to successful communication.

Chapter 14

Your Own Management Style

The most important things you can do as a manager are to know yourself, to understand what motivates the people around you, and to communicate effectively with others. It is equally important to know when you are communicating from your own place of stress and how to pull yourself out of it.

As a leader and manager, your attitude and approach will determine the outlook of everyone on your team. Whether you are upbeat or depressed, determined or resigned, accepting or skeptical, energetic or lethargic, optimistic or pessimistic—whatever your mind-set and attitude—it is contagious. You set the tone for everyone else.

HOW YOUR PERSONALITY TYPE AFFECTS YOUR MANAGEMENT STYLE

In this section, let's explore how personality affects management style. Take a moment to think about the type of manager you are. For example, do you want your team to participate in the decisions? Or do you prefer others to obey your orders without needing any explanations? Do you want your team members to manage themselves? Do you nurture and proactively support others?

Different types of personalities have different management styles. Let's look at four different management styles: Autocratic, Democratic, Laissez-Faire, and Paternalistic.

Autocratic

In the Autocratic management style, the manager retains the power and decision-making authority. An Autocratic manager does not typically consult or receive input from any other people. Instead, the team is expected to obey orders without the need for explanation. Autocratic managers motivate through a structured set of rewards and punishments.

Historically—especially in military and political contexts—Autocratic leadership has dominated management philosophy, but it has also been criticized over the past thirty years, particularly in management and leadership literature, as being overly harsh. Autocrats rely on threats and punishment and are usually not perceived as trusting their employees or subordinates. This style can be effective, however, when decision-making time is limited and quick, organized action is essential. Unsurprisingly, combat leadership is almost always executed in an Autocratic style.

This style can also be effective for executing rapid change. For example, if a manager has recently assumed leadership of a poorly managed team in danger of collapse, Autocratic decisions may be necessary to rescue it and get everyone back on track. Autocratic action may be required when a team questions a manager's authority; in such a case the manager may need to employ Autocratic methods to keep the team from deteriorating into mutiny. It should also be noted that Autocratic authority is almost always derived from organizational or hierarchical authority; subordinates cannot exercise Autocratic leadership of their superiors in an organization.

An Autocratic leadership style is usually necessary when team members do not understand tasks, procedures, or priorities. In such cases, the manager must make the decisions without input until the team has been trained and has gotten up to speed.

Democratic

The Democratic leadership style encourages all stakeholders to participate in the decision-making process. The Democratic manager keeps his or her team members and stakeholders informed about everything that affects their work, sharing decision-making and problem-solving responsibilities. This style requires the leader to have the final say, after first gathering information from all sources.

This style works best with highly skilled or experienced employees, when implementing operational changes, or when resolving individual or group problems.

Democratic leadership provides opportunities for employees to develop a high sense of personal growth and job satisfaction. It is also very effective when a large or complex problem requires input from many people for its solution. It creates "buy-in" from all stakeholders, thus fostering a sense of community and shared purpose.

Laissez-Faire

The Laissez-Faire leadership style is one in which the manager provides little or no direction and gives employees as much freedom as possible. Employees must determine goals, make decisions, and resolve problems on their own.

This style is effective only if the following conditions are met: team members are highly skilled and experienced; they are willing and able to make decisions for the success of the organization; the roles and responsibilities are clear; they know their roles; and little change is expected in expectations, time frames, or constraints.

Paternalistic

In the Paternalistic leadership style, the manager cares for, nurtures, and proactively takes responsibility to support others. Paternalistic leadership encourages open and honest communication, broad-based delegation, mutual trust, support, and respect for employees and coworkers. It concerns itself with fostering the organization's sense of community. Team members believe they are cared for; typically, they exhibit a sense of belonging to "a good team." This style typically keeps employee attrition low.

MISMANAGEMENT CHARACTERISTICS

Each individual manager tends to gravitate to one of these four management styles. Problems occur when the manager's style runs counter to their team's needs or situation. For example, if very rapid decisions are needed, a Democratic style would hinder the fast progress required.

The strongest leaders are able to apply each of the four management styles as the situation and team require.

Mismanagement takes many forms, including the following:

- Unwillingness to listen to employees

- Favoritism

- Diminishing employees

- Lack of decision-making

- Inappropriate behavior (e.g., sexual and racial harassment)

- Lack of respect toward employees

- Bullying or creating a fear-based environment

- Micro-managing, creating an environment of mistrust

Whatever the form, the result is a waste of the most important resource in business: the people. Mismanagement can cause discontent, low morale, and low sense of worth; it wastes time and individual productivity; and it loses money for the organization or project.

An Autocratic manager makes decisions unilaterally and may cause employees to sit back and wait for direction, become overly dependent on the manager, or become frustrated with the lack of trust and flexibility.

A Democratic manager may slow down the decision process too much because of their need for consensus.

A Laissez-Faire manager may evade the duties of management, resulting in uncoordinated delegation. The staff becomes unfocused, without a sense of direction, and dissatisfied.

A Paternalistic manager can mismanage by not making the tough decisions, not wanting to alienate people or risk having someone dislike them.

ADDRESSING YOUR OWN MISMANAGEMENT

When under stress, everyone can exhibit difficult personality behaviors. Pay attention to how you react to situations. The more you understand yourself, the more you will get insight on the part you play in relationship issues. Honestly ask yourself the following questions:

- Why am I reacting to this individual?

- How am I reacting?

- What emotions does this situation trigger in me?

Be introspective. Examine yourself and your behavior. Following are the common ways you can tell if you have slipped into the behavior of a difficult personality type:

- Manipulator: Withholding information or data from your team; blaming your team or other departments; taking credit for others' actions; showing up people in public; pitting people or teams against each other; being aggressive and bullying others.

- Gossiper: Talking about other people behind their backs; relishing the possession of information others do not have; using negative criticism of others to connect with people; targeting certain individuals you are unhappy with for criticism.

- Naysayer: Being sarcastic and critical; believing you are right and everyone else is wrong; focusing all your discussions and energy on what is wrong; not listening to others' opinions; resisting new ideas.

- Controller: Taking over discussions; being rigid about time and schedules; knowing what is best for every situation; not listening to others; not delegating or only delegating very small, specific tasks; wanting to be part of all decisions.

- Perfectionist: Taking on too much work; expecting perfection in yourself and in others; wanting to think for others; providing too much information; excessively redoing work; believing you can do everything better, faster, and more efficiently than others.

- Yes-Man: Feeling the need to please everyone; having a difficult time making decisions; becoming distraught and immobilized if there is conflict; over adapting to others; having difficultly saying no; taking situations personally; avoiding all conflict.

- Drama Queen: Wanting to be the center of attention; thriving on attention; exaggerating stories to make them more dramatic and engaging; betraying secrets of others; shifting moods; taking all conflicts and embellishing how it will affect you or your team.

- Recluse: Tuning out of discussions easily; ignoring your email and voice mail; starting tasks but not completing them; daydreaming often; struggling to prioritize multiple assignments.

- Whiner: Excessively complaining; placing blame on others; negativity.

- Liar: Telling untruths for some gain (respect, promotion, hiding actions); looking out for yourself and not your team or organization.

THE RIGHT APPROACH FOR THE SITUATION

High-functioning managers and leaders are able to adjust to different situations and use the right approach for each scenario. Stress makes high-functioning leadership difficult. To function at your maximum level, you must take steps to avoid becoming stressed and losing control.

No single communication style is better or worse than any other. However, some tasks and positions fit certain communication styles better than others. To have the most effective team, you should ideally have people with different communication styles in the appropriate positions.

Depending on the situation, each of the four management styles can be appropriate or be destructive. A good leader feels comfortable working in all four styles and applies the correct style to the situation and people. In any one day, it is possible to use Autocratic, Democratic, Laissez-Faire, and Paternalistic styles with different teams or situations. Practice using styles that are not as comfortable for you, as a way to increase your range of management skills.

Chapter Summary

There are four basic management styles: Autocratic, Democratic, Laissez-Faire, Paternalistic. Each management style has strengths and weaknesses dependent on the situation and team.

- What is your most comfortable style of management?
- Does it match the team you are leading?
- Are there any changes you can make to your style of management to make your team happier and more productive?

The most effective manager can switch between the management styles in response to the task and the team's abilities.

Chapter 15

Confrontation

If we lived in a perfect world, we could always identify problems with coworkers, bosses, and customers before they became critical, employ the perfect techniques to defuse the situation, and keep things moving along productively. However, since we live in the real world, we can count on conflict occasionally arising. We will encounter situations where we will need to know how and when to confront someone who obstructs the path of progress. Contrary to popular belief, however, confrontation isn't a dirty word. It doesn't have to be nasty, and it doesn't have to come with unpleasant aftereffects . . . but only if you do the work to make confrontation constructive.

> "Trying to get everyone to like you is a sign of mediocrity: you'll avoid the tough decisions, you'll avoid confronting the people who need to be confronted . . ."
> —Gen. (Ret) Colin Powell, US Secretary of State[1]

Communication sometimes requires confrontation. It is not a popular means of workplace communication, but sometimes confrontation must happen. Why does confrontation have such a negative connotation? Why is it uncomfortable to many people? Why do some people avoid it at all costs? Why does it often seem easier to handle problems via email instead of face-to-face?

Sometimes it demands tackling difficult or unpleasant issues head-on. Other times it involves discussing a topic with the expectation that the other party will respond badly or act out. Fortunately, it can be made less painful if you understand how to do it in a positive and effective manner.

> Confrontation is needed to resolve issues, but it does not have to be a negative experience.

One of the primary issues in communication is a misuse of confrontation: either it is completely avoided; attempted through indirect, back-channel means; or performed in a harsh and negative manner. Perhaps this shouldn't be surprising; the very word "confrontation" brings up all sorts of strong thoughts, beliefs, and emotions. So, let's talk about a way to confront that defuses much of the negativity and unpleasantness we often associate with the process.

COMPASSIONATE CONFRONTATION: IT'S NOT ALL ABOUT YOU

The type of confrontation you have depends on how much of your own ego you project into the situation. Once you understand the process of compassionate confrontation, much of the negativity can be removed, allowing the lines of communication to resume flowing much sooner.

First, let's define what is meant by "compassion."

Compassion is–

- Seeing the bigger picture
- Releasing your own ego, fear, and judgment while communicating with others

Compassion is not–

- Acceptance
- Sympathy
- Empathy
- Pity

Compassionate confrontation creates a common vision for going forward by presenting the issues in a way that the other person can hear. The goal of compassionate confrontation is not to produce separation but rather to create unity. Despite the negative response many of us have to the word "confrontation," when employed correctly, compassionate confrontation actually helps strengthen relationships.

Confronting someone from a place of anger, of course, is one of the worst and least productive ways to work through an issue. Anger is very disruptive and is usually born out of fear. A manager who confronts in anger may see short-term benefits, but negative lasting effects almost always ensue. When you are angry, step back; take the time to think through what needs to be said. Be sure to place your own focus on the issue at hand, not on your emotions, those of the other person, or especially your ego needs. In other words, you must defuse your feelings of stress before your communication can be effective.

Six practical steps can help you set up the calm, detached approach that fosters compassion and productive confrontation.

Compassionate Confrontation: Steps toward Success

1. Find common ground and determine a common goal for the meeting. Make sure the meeting is *only* about this goal.

2. Do not make a play for others' emotions, including those of the person you are confronting. Most people don't care what you feel, think, or believe—especially when they feel uneasy and stressed themselves. Focus the discussion on the issue—not personalities.

3. Make sure you understand your own reactions. What are you invested in? What are you reacting to? Being right? Being perfect? Doing things your way? Doing the least work you can? Making everyone on the team happy? Remember that in the vast majority of cases, people are not out to get you; they are simply protecting themselves from perceived negative circumstances.

4. During the confrontation, do not blame. Find a way to help the person save face. This doesn't mean you should not make your point, but you should be willing to give the other person a respectful way to renegotiate his or her position.

5. Do not project your feelings onto others. For example, avoid asserting that you "understand" them or their position on the issue. You almost never have the whole picture—especially from another person's perspective.

6. Present constructive options to the individual you are confronting. Creating a respectful way out of confrontation is an act of great maturity and enlightened leadership. Be careful, however, to avoid providing choices you don't have the authority to offer, that you don't really agree with, or that you know the other person won't agree to.

It's important to understand that compassion is not always warm and fluffy. Compassionate confrontation results from a leader having balance and a high degree of self-understanding. It is hard to confront in a productive manner when you are afraid, angry, or anxious.

Following are five vignettes that illustrate compassionate confrontation in situations with people in different roles and relationships. Scenarios one and two show a manager confronting a team member. The third scenario is a peer-to-peer confrontation. Scenario four is a confrontation with a boss, and scenario five involves a customer. In any confrontation, regardless of your role or that of the other person, you must take into account the personality type, situation, and relationship (see chapter 3) to engage in the most effective communication.

Martin, the retail warehouse manager, had heard through the grapevine that Rob, the shipping supervisor, was not happy. He felt Martin did not value his opinion on how to handle issues with the new inventory system. Martin made it a priority to find out what was up, knowing he needed to confront Rob before his disgruntled behavior affected the rest of the department.

Martin took some time to consider his approach, especially since there had been unproductive meetings between himself and Rob in the past. He hoped they could resolve their differences and feel good about the decisions that were made.

The next morning Martin scheduled a meeting in Rob's office, thinking that he would be more relaxed and at ease in his own space. Even though Martin didn't typically care much about details, he began by asking Rob his thoughts on how the new inventory system was working. Martin knew that listening to Rob's opinion would make him more comfortable and hopefully cultivate a new level of trust.

Having heard Rob's thoughts, Martin said, "Yeah, these are sound opinions. I'm concerned that the company can't afford to implement all of them, though. Can you think of a way to develop a cheaper but still effective solution?" Martin knew how much could be spent, but he felt it would benefit Rob to walk through the details and come up with the same final result on his own.

Rob discussed each change. He surprised Martin with an excellent solution to one issue that could save the company a lot of money. At the end of the meeting, Martin asked Rob to come to him directly if he had any further challenges with the system, rather than discussing them with other team members.

Martin knew that confronting Rob outright for his behavior would have been counterproductive, so he chose to set aside his personal agenda and fully listen. As a result, Rob felt valued and heard. He also learned something about the business, and Martin ended up with a better solution than he expected. Thanks to Martin's self-understanding, restraint, and display of respect, the meeting was win-win—and best of all, the company benefited.

Joe, the deputy project manager, had asked Bev, the chief engineer, for a summary of research on a new database technique. He had not given her a deadline but assumed she would provide it in a reasonable time frame. Now it had been over three weeks, and Joe had not received anything. He knew that if the assignment had been his, he would have developed a list of all the things he needed to do and finished some of the activities every day. Bev did not work that way. He needed to figure out a way to harness Bev's incredible creativity while impressing on her the importance of a set schedule.

Joe set up a meeting with Bev in his office, realizing that she felt uncomfortable having other people in her space. Bev arrived fifteen minutes late, which really bugged him. Worse, she did not apologize. Though annoyed, he decided not to say anything about it; he wanted this meeting to be focused on her database research and nothing else.

Joe started off the meeting chatting about the research. After a few minutes Bev admitted she had started the summary but then had gotten stalled. He surmised that her research had gone off on tangents and was not focused on the primary goals for the company. Joe took a deep breath. It was difficult for him not to blame or criticize Bev, since he was always so logical and organized. It was hard for him to understand how Bev worked.

In a calm voice, Joe talked to Bev about setting daily goals for her research. He had planned to lay out a two-week schedule but noticed from her body language that she seemed to shut down when he mentioned it. Thinking on his feet, he said, "Bev, tell me: How many days in advance are you comfortable planning?" Bev immediately perked up and said, without hesitation, "Three." They agreed to meet every three days for fifteen minutes to discuss the status of the project and plan the following three days. To Joe's surprise, Bev looked relieved to have a schedule and daily milestones.

Joe ended the meeting by talking about the details of her research. Joe loved to hear about new technology, and he realized that Bev's incredible ability to bring disparate research together held exciting potential for the company. They chatted for thirty more minutes. Bev walked out of the meeting feeling that she had someone she could really talk to about her research. The daily schedule milestones gave her a set of specific goals to work toward. She printed out the schedule and hung it on her office door so she would see it every day.

After Bev left, Joe felt great about the project's potential and looked forward to talking to her on a regular basis.

Linda, the software development manager, was having difficulties with Jan, the test manager. They had a good relationship, but lately Jan was angry at the software team and blaming them for her problems.

Linda cared deeply for her team's well-being, so Jan's behavior disturbed her. Being very intuitive, Linda tried hard to get to know each person on her project; she realized Jan hated sitting in meetings. Unfortunately, there had been a lot of meetings recently. Each time, Jan frequently shifted positions and played with her phone. Linda could tell Jan was getting tense and angry.

Linda wanted to get Jan out of the office and relaxed before talking to her about the situation. She knew Jan liked playing laser tag and took her team to play about once a month as a team-building exercise. One evening, she took Jan to play a round and order a pizza. Linda didn't really enjoy all the running and the loud music, but it seemed to get Jan jazzed up and engaged. Over dinner, Linda probed Jan about how life was going. "I'm bored," Jan admitted. "I've been doing the same job for a while. All the meetings drive me crazy. I need something new to do!"

Linda and Jan starting brainstorming ideas to update Jan's job. They started out with reasonable ideas, but their suggestions became more and more outlandish; in about ten minutes, both were laughing uncontrollably. At the end of the meal, they agreed to meet the next day to work out specifics on how Linda could give Jan more interesting and exciting work to do.

Frank's boss, Ralph, did everything at the last minute. There was always a lot of drama surrounding the "crisis du jour." Frank would meet all his deadlines, but Ralph rarely looked at a presentation, email, or report until the last minute. He would then keep Frank at work until late at night making hurried changes or updates. Frank had tried requesting early feedback, but Ralph kept doing everything in crisis mode; he seemed to love the intensity and drama of a frantic environment. It made Frank mad to be kept at work so many nights and weekends for things that could have easily been completed earlier during normal hours.

Frank knew he needed to confront Ralph before these feelings caused Frank to lash out. The next day Ralph gave him an assignment that was due in one week, and saw this as an opportunity to change the pattern. He finished the assignment—a presentation for company executives—and requested an hour to meet the next day with Ralph.

When Frank started the meeting, he stated that he wanted to review the presentation. Ralph changed the topic to other things on his mind. Frank said politely, "I don't want to work late this week or on the weekend. I need this reviewed today so I can have that time with my family."

After reviewing a few pages, Ralph said he would look at the presentation on Friday and give feedback then. Frank stood his ground. "It would be better to finish now, please." He carefully avoided mention or display of emotions. He knew he was changing a pattern Ralph had followed for a long time; it was important to keep to the topic and not allow Ralph any opportunity to create drama.

Somewhat reluctantly, Ralph continued to look at the presentation and gave Frank the comments he wanted. Frank thanked Ralph for his prompt attention and told him how much he appreciated his comments. For his next three assignments, Frank set up a similar meeting with Ralph.

Marcia was managing a contract designed to deliver a complex interactive museum display to the local science center, and she had just received what felt like the one hundredth request for change. Many things the customer, Janet, wanted were just not doable. Worse, she seemed to have no idea about the impact of these requests on the schedule. Marcia had explained many times that the changes really taxed her team and they were working many extra hours.

Marcia needed to keep Janet happy because other large contracts up for bid fell under Janet's authority. Feeling Janet would be more comfortable in her own office, Marcia scheduled the meeting there. Knowing Janet was extremely detail-oriented, she started the meeting by praising Janet for her organization and time-management skills. She showed Janet the detailed schedule, the status, and the milestones completed, saying, "We are in the process of ordering all the material. Any additional changes will incur additional cost." Marcia refrained from talking about how frustrated her team was, the long hours they were putting in, and how angry they all were. Instead, she stuck with the facts and details and did not inject any emotion to the discussion.

She said, "Janet, your comments are always helpful. We think the end result will be a very functional, appealing display. We can't accept additional change requests if we're going to be ready for the scheduled opening night. Let's go over the detailed schedule once more." She wanted to be sure Janet would truly understand that there wasn't any more slack left in the delivery timeline.

Janet thanked Marcia for coming in, stated that she understood that they couldn't accept any additional changes, and requested a detailed schedule update every week. Marcia promised to send twice-weekly updates and to schedule weekly check-ins. Marcia then went back to her desk, wrote out an email detailing the discussion and their agreement, and sent it to Janet.

As you can see, in each case the initiator of the confrontation focused the discussion on the facts rather than venting or satisfying personal ego needs. This is perhaps the most important aspect of compassionate confrontation: The confronter must have sufficient self-understanding to avoid acting while stressed or out of control. He must also be perceptive of the other individual's personality needs in order to structure communication for optimal reception. Remember, compassionate confrontation isn't about you, the initiator; it's about the facts and the communication situation. Once you realize this, you can remove much of the negative emotion from the equation and focus on what you really want: communicating effectively to remove the roadblocks to success. When you can do that, you'll be well on your way to becoming the type of high-performing manager and leader that you aspire to be.

Chapter Summary

Compassionate confrontation is a critical technique for effective communication and leadership. Compassion is defined as seeing the big picture and releasing your own ego, fear, and judgment while communicating with others. Compassionate confrontation creates a common vision for going forward by presenting the issues and direction in a unifying manner.

The worst, least productive way to work through an issue is to confront others from a place of anger. Anger is usually born out of fear. A manager that confronts using anger may see a short-term benefit, but the negative effects are long lasting.

- Do you confront people in anger?

- How can you change the way you confront people to create more unity and teamwork?

There are six steps to use during confrontation:

1. Determine a common goal for the meeting, and make sure the meeting is only about that goal.

2. Focus the discussion on the issue and not on your emotions.

3. Make sure you understand why you are reacting.

4. Do not blame. Find a way for the person to save face.

5. Do not project your feelings onto others.

6. Create a respectful environment and present constructive options.

Chapter 16

Leadership

Now that we have learned techniques to communicate effectively with all different types of people, using different styles and mediums; how to present yourself and listen and respond to others; and how to resolve conflict in a way that fosters greater teamwork and keeps your organization moving toward its goals, let's put it all together so you can be a great leader people will remember.

What makes you want to follow or work for one person and not another? Whom do you remember as the best leader you ever followed? What was (or is) the nature of that leader's character? What made this leader so special?

> Great leaders get ordinary
> people and teams to do
> **extraordinary things.**

As we try to tie together everything we've discussed about leading various personality types, let's take advantage of some of the wisdom available from great leaders and students of leadership. Throughout this chapter, you'll see quotes and advice from those who have devoted years of study to the question of what makes leaders effective. I hope you'll take advantage of these as points of reflection and inspiration for further study and improvement of your own leadership "toolbox."

There are many definitions of leadership. Organizational consultant and scholar Warren Bennis states, "Leadership is a function of knowing yourself, having a vision that is well communicated, building trust among colleagues, and taking effective action to realize your own leadership potential."[1] Bennis's definition describes the fundamentals of leadership: vision, trust, and good communication.

Successful leaders exhibit the following five traits:

1. They know themselves.

2. They establish vision and direction.

3. They empower their teams.

4. They align people in positions to maximize each individual's strengths.

5. They consistently motivate and inspire.

Let's take a closer look at each of these attributes, especially as they apply to successfully communicating with stakeholders as a team leader.

1. KNOWING YOURSELF

Know Your Personal Ego Needs

Leaders are more effective if they make decisions without the influence of their egos and judgments about people or situations. Individual ego needs produce blind spots and cloud judgment. The more you know yourself and the part you play in relationship issues, the easier it is to be nonjudgmental, objective, and fair.

A leader's ego can also present itself as fear. This fear—of failure, loss of status, lack of recognition, or other factors—translates into destructive actions such as always needing to be right, verbally attacking others, indecision, failure to delegate, withdrawing, risk aversion, or taking inappropriate risks.

To start learning about yourself, pay attention to how you react throughout your day. Ask yourself these questions:

- Why do certain people trigger reactions in me?
- When do I feel angry?
- What part of me feels threatened, and why?

Continue to Grow as a Leader

In order to remain effective, leaders must continue to grow. Every situation you encounter as a leader or a team member presents you with a growth opportunity. This includes occasions when something doesn't work out the way you planned. History demonstrates clearly that everyone fails from time to time. The distinguishing feature of great leaders is that following failure, they know how to get up, keep going, and learn from their mistakes.

As the people with whom you associate most closely day in and day out, your team will not fail to see your process in action as you work on yourself and make needed changes. Don't be afraid to be appropriately vulnerable to your team; let them see that you recognize your flaws and that you are willing to change. A leader who can admit shortcomings without becoming paralyzed by self-doubts will serve as a powerful example for any team.

Your personal growth plan can start with a simple three-step strategy:

1. Request and receive regular feedback from a trusted mentor.

2. Do a "personal lessons learned" introspection every week that includes these questions:

   a. What went well?

   b. What could I have done better?

   c. When did my ego cause me to not listen or to handle a situation badly?

3. Meet monthly with the leadership on your team and do a group evaluation of the past thirty days.

2. ESTABLISHING VISION AND DIRECTION

Develop a Vision for the Future and Strategies for Producing Changes

Change is continuous, but sometimes it can be difficult. Even positive change can present complications, requiring shifts in thought and process. A manager must provide a clear vision in order to ensure successful change. You must maintain a clear sense of the final destination that will endure despite temporary shifts in course.

The leader's vision is the team's road map to success. What defines success for your team: Having happy users of your product? Meeting financial goals? Hiring twenty people? Meeting cost and schedule goals? Responding swiftly to changing customer requirements? Whatever spells success in your organization, it is up to you as leader to articulate that and to keep it constantly in the forefront of everyone's efforts. Without a vision, how can any enterprise or team know where it is headed? How can people make correct decisions without knowing the end goal? Theodore Hesburg sums it up nicely: "The very essence of leadership is that you have to have vision. You can't blow an uncertain trumpet."[2]

Communicate the Vision by Words and Deeds

A leader needs to communicate the vision in both written and verbal media. A good leader embraces the vision, lives the vision, and becomes a champion of the vision.

Every decision and discussion should be put in context of the vision for the organization and its success criteria. As you look at priorities and assign activities, ask yourself, "How do these activities line up with our success criteria?" Activities that do not line up should be avoided or redesigned.

Facilitate Completion

A good leader understands how to bring a task to completion, first of all by defining what it means for an activity, document, or product to be complete. People need to know they have successfully completed a task in order to become fully involved with the next one. Even in a chaotic environment, when requirements and priorities are constantly changing, it is important to have a structure that allows teams to feel a sense of accomplishment. There are many ways to define completion; sometimes, for example, completion is defined as simply meeting the requirements within cost and schedule objectives. However, sometimes the concept of completion must take into account more complex factors such as customer satisfaction.

Develop a Plan Consistent with Your Goals and Requirements

While this sounds obvious, it is amazing how many management approaches and associated plans are designed counter to the vision and goals of the organization or company.

"Leadership is the capacity to translate vision into reality."

–WARREN G. BENNIS[3]

Know and understand the goals and requirements of your organization and stakeholders. Goals can be things like maximizing profits, creating the best product to gain market share, diversifying the business customer base, or having superior user satisfaction. As a leader, you need to know exactly what the goals are. Where you put your resources and energy will shift depending on your goals.

It is imperative that a leader communicates to the team, to the organization, and to management the priorities and the vision of the organization. When focused on priorities and clear on the vision, each person on the team will be able to make decisions to maximize the goals of the organization.

3. EMPOWERING YOUR TEAM

Push Down Responsibility and Authority to Empower the Team to Make Decisions

One of the worst things that can happen is for decisions not to be made, or for all the decisions to be made by the manager. How discouraging! Such an organization typically grinds to a halt when the leader is out; teams become disgruntled; and personnel with innovative ideas and self-motivation leave the organization.

There is a significant difference, however, between micromanaging and leveraging control. Micromanagement is telling the team *how* to do the job; leveraging control tells the team *what* they need to do. The difference between telling the team how to do the task and what to do is huge. There is a time and place for micromanagement, but it should only happen for specific reasons and short bursts of time.

"The best executive is the one who has sense enough to pick good
men to do what he wants done and self-restraint to keep from
meddling with them while they do it."

–THEODORE ROOSEVELT[1]

How can you create an environment that will allow and accommodate the appropriate sharing of decision-making responsibility? First, your team must operate in an atmosphere of trust.

Provide an Environment of Trust

What does an environment of trust gain you?

Trust encourages teams to work together to solve problems. When a team has a culture of trust, both from management toward the team and vice versa, there will be more disclosure of information, more acceptance of others' ideas, and a more comfortable, relaxed, and creative atmosphere.

In an environment of trust, ideas are encouraged and fostered. Work becomes exciting because people feel as if they are part of the solution. Trust is an amazing teambuilding tool.

An environment of trust starts with the manager. If the team, customer, or upper management senses hidden agendas, withholding of information, or lies, they will hold back in turn. Trust is a self-reinforcing process.

How do you create a trusting environment?

Share information so that people are not forced to make assumptions, and be honest in your communication. It's that simple.

In Steven Gaffney's wonderful book *Just Be Honest*, he describes a communication strategy he calls "Notice vs. Imagine."

The problem is not that we have assumptions, conclusions, evaluations, and opinions; that's a normal part of being a human being. The problem lies in thinking that we are right and not checking in to verify that our imaginations are correct.[5]

Steven Gaffney estimates that at least 50 percent of what we imagine about others is inaccurate.

For example, upon exiting a meeting at work, 50 percent of our thoughts, opinions, and assumptions are likely to be wrong. When another person leaves the meeting 50 percent of his thoughts, opinions, and assumptions are likely to be wrong as well. If each person does not take the time to check in with his or her own imaginations, the result is two different people who received two totally different messages from the same meeting! The worse part about this is that each person may well think he or she is 100 percent right.[6]

The only way to create a trusting environment is to communicate frequently, openly, and honestly.

4. MAXIMIZING INDIVIDUAL STRENGTHS

Know Your Team and Their Talents

Analyze your team members and find out their natural talents and skills. Take the time to learn who on your team is good at seeing the big picture, who is good at completion, and who is good at understanding details. Realign your staff to take advantage of these different skills.

Mark was doing a poor job in team management and leadership. The chief operating officer (COO) and president discussed firing him, but the COO felt Mark's knowledge and vision were valuable to the organization.

His talents were in seeing the big picture, communicating the vision to the customer, and providing guidance to the team on how to meet the vision. However, Mark did not like or perform well at detail-oriented tasks. The COO decided to replace Mark as a team leader but made him a technical expert in the organization. Subsequently, Mark became one of the most valuable members of the team and proved vital to the successful completion of multiple projects. If Mark had been fired without analyzing his talents and envisioning how to use them for the benefit of the organization, the end result would have been far less satisfactory. Leadership found the right place for Mark to be successful, and he, in turn, helped make the organization more successful.

Aligning people based on their talents requires flexibility, initiative, and energy. The alternative, however, is a team that doesn't trust its leadership.

Define Clear Authority and Accountability

How do you feel when you don't know who has the authority to make a decision?

When no one is accountable, what happens to the goals?

As a leader, you need to provide clear roles and responsibilities. Be very clear when you state who has the authority and the responsibility for major activities.

One of the worst situations to be put in is to have the responsibility for a task but no real authority. Putting team members in such a bind can be frustrating and destructive.

An expert was brought in to a troubled project to do a rapid assessment and implement change. What she found was a manager who was given all the responsibility to run the project but no authority to make things happen. The chief financial officer (CFO), who was the project manager's supervisor, would come to his daily team meetings and make detailed decisions. To make matters worse, the project manager was not allowed to make any staffing changes without consent of the CFO. So, when things went wrong, the project manager got the blame; when things went right, the CFO took the credit.

It turned out that the project manager was very good but had not been allowed to do his job. The expert recognized the issue and worked with the company to clearly draw the lines of authority and responsibility for the project manager. Subsequently, the project started getting back on track.

5. MOTIVATING AND INSPIRING

Show Passion and Excitement

A passionate leader will promote passion and excitement throughout the team.

Take a moment to think about whom you would rather work for: a manager who is excited and happy about coming to work each day or a manager who is indifferent and distracted. It has been observed that a team with great passion and commitment, but inferior resources and equipment, will almost always outperform a team with a ho-hum attitude, even if the latter team has state-of-the-art equipment and resources. As a leader, it's up to you to exhibit a sense of excitement and anticipation about what you are doing. This attitude is contagious— and that's a good thing.

Help People Energize Themselves to Overcome Barriers to Change

Change happens effectively when people get excited about it and its benefits. However, any change, no matter how small, requires a transition. As William Bridges stated so well in his book *Managing Transitions*, "It isn't the changes that do you in, it's the transition."[7]

He outlines three phases of a transition:

1. Letting go of the old ways and old identity people had.

2. Going through an in-between time when the old is gone but the new isn't fully operational.

3. Coming out of the transition and making a new beginning.

Even team members who embrace the change will go through these three steps. One of the most effective ways to facilitate a transition is through frequent communication. A lack of clear information can create a lot of disinformation, which is disruptive and destructive.

On occasion, there will be people on the team who, despite your best efforts at communicating through the transition, will continue to be disruptive, resist change, and discount new ideas. They become the center of negative energy flowing through the organization. They constantly complain and undermine the leader's authority. Unless you can get these individuals functioning from a better place, they can poison the health of your organization. The maxim "One bad apple ruins the batch" applies to organizations as well as produce. In such cases, there are two primary options open to a manager:

1. Work to move the individual(s) out of fear. This is always the best option in the beginning. However, if the benefit you receive from having the person in the organization does not outweigh

the amount of time you spend dealing with the backlash of this person's behavior, it is time to take a more drastic move.

2. Move them out of the organization. This is the easiest and quickest way to "fix" a disruptive personnel problem. However, sometimes it can cause unintended change by either starting a wave of people leaving the organization or creating a knowledge gap. Always weigh carefully the costs and benefits of removing or replacing a team member.

Chapters 4–13 describe communicating with difficult people. It is imperative that the manager communicate frequently with disruptive individuals. In this way, even if the decision is to move them off the team, it can be done in a way that benefits both the individual and the team. Chapter 15 describes confrontation techniques to help you create a common goal and resolve issues without ego displays or undue emotional disruption.

Be a Role Model for Ethical Behavior

The manager sets the culture and tone of the organization and team. If the leader sets a high ethical standard, the culture becomes one of similarly high standards.

But why is it important to have an organization with high ethical standards? What does it mean to be involved in an ethical organization or team? How do you set and maintain a high ethical standard?

Ethics is the process of determining right and wrong. Organizations with high ethical standards are characterized by honesty, clarity, and openness. Risks of all types are reduced, because collaboration and honest discussion typify the team, from top to bottom.

As a manager, you need to show the team, by your words and actions, what is right or wrong. If the team sees you lying to your manager or customer or cutting corners, they will assume that type of behavior is acceptable. If team members see you take home office supplies, waste time with non-company-related online pursuits, or do personal activities on company time, they will assume these behaviors are acceptable for them as well. This can cost any team valuable time and money.

Of course, it is easiest to behave ethically when things are going well. Good people who believe they are ethical will sometimes behave unethically when an organization, company, or project gets in trouble. The most common example of this is lying about the status of a task. However, people have to know about issues in order to help fix them. A team who hides or lies about status is in big trouble—not to mention ineffective. To resolve this—

- Keep communication open.

- Keep listening.

- Actively manage risks.

Open discussion and management of risks promote honesty and clarity.

Remember That Positive Energy Creates More Positive Energy

Think about whom you want to work for: A boss who is energetic, believes in the organization, and is optimistic about the future? Or a boss who is pessimistic and complains?

Positive—and, unfortunately, negative—energy from a leader permeates throughout the organization. A wave of positive energy pulls people together, makes them believe in their mission, increases productivity, and saves money and time.

Negative energy from a leader creates more negative energy. The team spends time complaining, whining, and not focusing on success. Such teams typically end up over budget and past deadlines.

Colin Powell, one of the great leaders of our country, wrote:

The ripple effect of a leader's enthusiasm and optimism is awesome. So is the impact of cynicism and pessimism. Leaders who whine and blame engender those same behaviors among their colleagues. I am not talking about stoically accepting organizational stupidity and performance incompetence with a "what, me worry?" smile. I am talking about a gung ho attitude that says, "We can change things here, we can achieve awesome goals, we can be the best." Spare me the grim litany of the "realist"; give me the unrealistic aspirations of the optimist any day.[8]

Attitudes Are Contagious: Are Yours Worth Catching?[9]

Care about Your Team
Have you ever had a boss you believed really cared about you? How did it make you feel? Didn't you work harder for that person? This may not mean your boss wasn't tough or demanding—just that he or she truly cared. How can you show you care as a manager?

Listen to Your Team Members
You can learn so much by listening more and talking less. Keep your ego in check, and don't assume that everyone wants to listen to you talk.

There may be extraordinary ideas, opinions, and thoughts you miss . . . just by failing to listen.

Chapter Summary

Great leaders project a sense of caring to each team member. They genuinely concern themselves with the welfare of those they lead, realizing that people are the most important part of any organization.

- What can you change in your leadership style to create a more productive, happy, and unified team?
- How can you show your team you care?
- Do you have a vision and direction that you have communicated to your team?
- Have you empowered your team and put personnel in the positions that align with their strengths?

In an atmosphere of caring and mutual trust, great leaders operate with transparency, honesty, and the highest ethics. Great leaders know themselves; they establish a vision and direction; they empower their team; they align team members according to individual strengths; and they motivate and inspire.

Become a great leader people will remember!

Chapter 17

Next Steps

Effective communication unites teams and provides a framework for a vision and goal to be met. To be a good leader, you must be able to communicate effectively to all different types of people, using different styles and mediums. This book has taught you how to adapt your communication in order to work with various types of individuals, how to present yourself, how to listen and respond to others, how to recognize stress in yourself and others, and how to resolve conflict in a way that fosters greater teamwork and keeps teams moving toward goals.

The fact is, almost everything you will ever accomplish in your life—in work, at home, even with your favorite hobby—is made possible, one way or another, by the efforts of other people. To be a world-class leader, your ability to motivate, inspire, and above all communicate effectively with other people will determine how successful you are able to become. Long-term, year in and year out, the top performers are those who are able to get the most out of every member of their teams. And to do that, you've got to be able to communicate.

Let's take a quick tour through the main principles we've covered in this book.

1. COMMUNICATION IS THE CORNERSTONE OF EFFECTIVE MANAGEMENT AND LEADERSHIP.

We learned that effective communication unites teams and provides a framework for a vision and a goal to be met. Everything in life is about communication and relationships; management is no exception. Knowing how to motivate your team members by utilizing their strengths will help you have a high-functioning team so your organization will meet its goals.

2. EACH COMMUNICATION TOOL HAS DIFFERING COMMUNICATION CAPABILITIES.

The communication methods available to you as a manager and leader offer particular advantages and disadvantages, depending on the situation and persons involved.

Face-to-face (including video teleconferencing) and **telephone** communication are more personal than email and texting, because they involve tone of voice, facial expression, and other nonverbal cues that greatly aid in the accurate sending and receiving of information. Also for this reason, they are slower and more time consuming. Active listening skills let the other person know you are attending carefully to what is being said. With telephone conversations, it is especially important to monitor your tone of voice and to use polite expressions such as "please" and "thank you," since your communication partner is unable to see your face or body language. On the phone, be sure to identify yourself clearly to anyone you are calling, and state the reason for your call early in the conversation, to avoid confusion and wasted time.

Email and **texting** are almost instantaneous, enabling you to send a message to a single individual or a large group of people, even if they are in different places. However, as with most things, the method's greatest strength is also its greatest weakness. Because email and text messages can be composed and sent so quickly—and especially because they are sent and received without attributes such as facial expression, body language, or tone of voice—they require careful thought to be sure that the message is communicated accurately. Even interoffice email and text messages should use correct grammar and should never contain negative or potentially sensitive information about another person, since they can be forwarded to recipients you never intended. Similarly, emails and text messages should never be used for confrontation or processing of communication that could involve strong negative emotions; such matters are better addressed face-to-face or, as a second resort, in a telephone call.

Meetings and **presentations**, both group and individual, are an important fact of life in most offices and enterprises. Now, thanks to telecommunication technology, these can also include video- and teleconferences with people in remote locations. Whatever form your meeting or presentation takes, it is paramount that you have a clear agenda for the meeting—preferably a written one—and that everyone present knows the purpose of the meeting and its desired outcome, whenever possible. Have your materials and equipment organized and prepared ahead of time, especially if you are using audiovisual elements. Be prepared to deal with questions or discussions that could derail the progress of the event, so that you can lead the attendees through the agenda, keeping the meeting on track.

Written reports may be contractually required elements for a project or written status for the board of directors, or they may be requested by a supervisor in response to a special need or situation. In either case, the report should clearly match the importance of its purpose, and it should also be continually evaluated—especially in the case of recurring reports—to be certain that it continues to be useful and relevant for its recipients. All reports must employ correct grammar and usage and ideally should be proofread by someone other than the preparer prior to presentation.

3. EFFECTIVE COMMUNICATION TAKES INTO ACCOUNT THE SITUATION, RELATIONSHIP, AND PERSONALITY.

Remember that each communication event, regardless of the form used, has three elements: the situation, the relationship between the parties, and the personalities of the people involved. Situations can be formal or informal, anything from a gathering with coworkers after working hours to a one-on-one presentation given to a prospective client. The parties communicating may be employees at the same level in an organization, a supervisor and a subordinate, a customer and a vendor, or anything in between. Each individual has certain personality attributes that lend themselves to particular formats and styles of communication, and as a manager, it's up to you to know what to use, with whom, and when.

4. CONFRONT DETRIMENTAL BEHAVIORS AND WORK AT CHANGING DESTRUCTIVE HABITS.

Manipulator—Manipulation can show up in many different ways in the workplace, creating a toxic environment. Manipulators are often bullies and, by using devious methods, control others. Manipulators often create a chaotic emotional situation allowing the exploitation of others. Manipulators are reacting to fear they are not enough, fear they are not competent.

Manipulators are controlling, so it is critical to find a way to take away some of that control in a positive way. Ask probing questions that point out that they are only looking at the picture from one side. For example: Can you help me understand how this benefits the program?

With bullies, remain firm. Call their bluff by gently and calmly exposing the fallacies in their statements. Use a direct, no-nonsense approach to reveal their deceptions. The bully has achieved their goal if you get flustered or rattled. Don't become their victim. We are manipulated because we allow it, and refusing to be manipulated is the first step.

Gossiper—Gossip is rampant in most workplaces. People speculate about everything.

You need to act on gossip if it's disrupting the workplace, causing morale issues, or hurting employees. Gossiping can create a toxic culture, causing mistrust and lower morale.

When communicating with a Gossiper, please keep in mind that the Gossiper may feel anxious about his or her place in the organization. It is better to use a coaching approach to the situation—it is a habit the person needs to break. Use a nonconfrontational approach but one that makes it clear you believe the gossip is negative and harmful. The person may or may not understand the harm that is being done.

Naysayer—Naysayers say why things cannot or should not be done. They question every decision and have strong opinions. Naysayers focus on the flaws of the situation.

Naysayers want to feel they have been heard. If you ignore them or marginalize them, they will only become louder and more disruptive. A Naysayer comes across blustery and strong but is typically very sensitive and has a deep need to be right. When talking to a Naysayer, keep the discussion on the facts and stay away from your opinions. Listen to their view of the facts. Try to use words that do not convey emotions or judgments. Many times, Naysayers have good ideas, but their approach and method of voicing their ideas is disruptive. When Naysayers are backed into a corner, they dig in and stop listening. Provide Naysayers with a safe place to discuss their opinions and the facts of the situation; give them face-saving opportunities to change their minds without feeling any outside judgment.

Controller—Controllers want things done the "right way." And, of course, the way to do, act, think, and speak is their way. They are interested not just in the outcome but in how you get to the end goal.

Controllers are motivated by power and exercising influence over others. They don't delegate well and get frustrated with others.

Controllers typically do not value emotions. Provide details to help lower anxiety levels. Do not respond with emotion to their controlling. Do not take it personally when they are controlling. Their control compulsion is not about you. The less you react to their incitements, the more objective you can be. Make it a point to give praise and recognize their contributions to the workplace. Controllers typically view things as strictly black and white—things are good or bad, right or wrong. Put things in writing so you can be clear and concise, protect yourself from sabotage, and make sure the expectations are clear on both sides. Stand up to a Controller without being confrontational. They do not react well to a direct challenge. Stay calm and controlled while talking to a Controller.

Perfectionist—Perfectionists are typically goal oriented and expect perfection in themselves and others. Perfectionists are driven by their fear of failure and may conceal mistakes because of fear of judgment. Perfectionists typically take on too much work. A Perfectionist wants to think for others, usually provides too much information, and is easily frustrated about perceptions of equity, fairness, and order.

To keep a Perfectionist working at the optimum level, compliment him or her on their organizational skills and accomplishments. Keep a Perfectionist focused on the schedule, otherwise they will continuously redo work (their work and others'). Achievement is important to them and they need not only to recognize their own work but also to have others recognize it and express appreciation for it.

Yes-Man—Yes-Men are always trying to please the people around them and will usually do what is asked (or what they *assume* is asked) without question. They instinctively avoid conflict and become stressed when disharmony occurs. The danger with having a Yes-Man in your organization is that they are motivated primarily to keep the peace and not necessarily to ensure the organization's success.

These individuals must have a trusted, safe place to discuss difficult issues. Yes-Men should not be blamed for bringing up problems. Instead, they need warm conversations and gentle leading up to the point of the conversation. Yes-Men prefer face-to-face conversations but will respond to email, text, and meetings as long as these are not abrupt or abrasive. Yes-Men tend to be nurturing and easily acknowledge their feelings.

Drama Queen—There is a Drama Queen in every team. This person thrives on attention, spins small issues into disasters, always tops your stories with a tale of their own, and wants to be the center of attention. Drama Queens can take minor conflicts as personal affronts; will blame others if they screw up; have dramatic mood shifts; dominate any social gathering; and will overshare. The Drama Queens want to be in the thick of activities and act like a victim.

Keep the discussion to facts. Drama Queens tend to exaggerate, blow things out of proportion, and editorialize. Don't get sucked into the drama. Ask the Drama Queen to summarize what happened in one sentence. That will force them to get to the facts of the issue. Repeat back the facts that you heard, taking out all emotion, empathy, and compassion. Ask the Drama Queen what they can do about the issue. This pushes the actions back to them. Don't tell them what to do, as this simply continues the drama. Just listen, and ask what actions they can take to resolve the issue.

Recluse—Recluses are typically reflective and imaginative and are often the creative engine of many revolutionary ideas. However, they typically do not do well implementing their ideas. They often become overwhelmed and have difficulty prioritizing multiple assignments. Recluses need time alone to think and process. They are not motivated by schedules and time constraints; instead, they tune out. Recluses withdraw when there are too many people around or there is too much pressure.

Recluses typically withdraw when communication involves anger, threats, or attacks. When talking to a Recluse, the conversation should be nonthreatening in order to permit the Recluse to reflect and think. Know in advance that detailed administrative tasks will not get done. Recluses do not mind at all if other people do all the administrative tasks and make decisions.

Whiner—Whiners moan, complain, grumble, and blame others for all their difficulties. It takes emotional energy to fend off the negative energy of someone's constant complaints, making people around the Whiner less productive. Whiners can drag down an organization because the negativity can be "catching," and soon your whole organization is thinking about what is wrong instead of what is going right.

When talking to the Whiner, ask them to help you develop a solution. Sometimes Whiners can point out real issues in an organization. Empower them to help fix the issues and to be invested in changes. If they are part of the solution, their whining will diminish. Keep the conversation positive and lively, if at all possible. Many times, Whiners don't see how their behavior impacts the organization.

Liar—Liars tell untruths. People lie for a variety of reasons: to build up their own image, to cover up an action, to spare people's feelings, to manipulate others, to put others down, to be more likable, to prevent a conflict or negative reaction to a situation, to justify a behavior, to appear more competent, or to avoid consequences of their actions.

When talking to a Liar, pay close attention to the details of what they are saying. Repeat their statements so they know you are paying attention. Follow up with an email documenting every detail of the conversation. Try to understand what motivates the Liar so you can work on solving the underlying problem. Be careful about jumping to conclusions as to who is telling the truth. Practiced Liars are believable and typically seem trustworthy. Pay attention to body language that doesn't match the words being stated to identify untruths.

5. IT'S IMPORTANT TO KNOW YOUR MANAGEMENT STYLE.

Never forget that just as the people you work with have their own personality styles and ways of sending and receiving communication, you do too. Knowing how you react in certain situations will enable you to anticipate and adapt both your communication and leadership styles for maximum positive effect.

The primary leadership styles are—

- Autocratic—dictatorial, directive, "top-down"; often used in military situations, when a team is in danger of collapse, or when team members are very inexperienced and require frequent supervision.
- Democratic—participatory; gathers information from all stakeholders before making decisions. Works best with an experienced team.
- Laissez-Faire—little or no direction given; team members proceed on their own. Works best with a very experienced team.
- Paternalistic—nurturing, broad-based; proceeds from sense of community and consensus.

To be a truly skilled leader and manager, you must be able to move among the various leadership styles, since each may be the best approach for a different situation. Knowing your personality type and inclinations will help you make purposeful, informed choices about the best strategies to employ, rather than simply doing what feels most comfortable. By learning yourself and your preferences for communication, you can exercise discernment and choose proactively how to best proceed.

6. USE COMPASSIONATE CONFRONTATION TECHNIQUES TO SOLVE PROGRAM COMMUNICATION ISSUES.

Just as good leadership sometimes necessitates dealing with people under stress, it also sometimes necessitates confronting people in order to get the organization back on track and moving in a productive direction. But remember: confrontation doesn't have to be a negative experience. Instead, using the principles of "compassionate confrontation," you can convert the crisis into an opportunity for growth, both for yourself and for the person you are confronting.

Compassionate confrontation involves recognizing that your own ego and emotional needs are not the primary focus. Instead, see the bigger picture, and resist the urge to judge, label, or blame as you communicate with the other person. By doing this, you can create a shared vision and a unified effort, without depriving the team or enterprise of your or the other person's strengths, abilities, and experiences.

When you must confront someone, have a goal clearly in mind—something concrete, factual, and unrelated to personalities or egos. Make sure you proceed with this goal in mind, and keep all other matters off the agenda. Avoid blaming, assigning motives, or discussing other persons. Do not assert feelings—even your own—and give the other person every opportunity to save face. Make every effort to present constructive, feasible options rather than insisting on a single alternative. Remember that compassionate confrontation isn't about proving who's in charge; it's about removing roadblocks and moving ahead in an environment of respect and open communication.

7. BECOME A GREAT LEADER PEOPLE WILL REMEMBER.

As you think back on leaders you remember and admire, consider the traits that made them great. Think about the attributes of quality leadership that we discussed in this book:

1. Great leaders know themselves; they understand their own strengths and weaknesses and especially how these fit in with the strengths and weaknesses of the people on their team.

2. Great leaders establish vision and direction; they are able to articulate what must be done in a way that clearly communicates to others, and they are able to encourage others to join in realizing a vision.

3. Great leaders empower their teams; they push down responsibility and accountability, and they make sure that team members have the proper resources to accomplish the tasks they have been given.

4. Great leaders align team members in accordance with individual strengths; they recognize the unique gifts of their team members and do everything possible to position them for success.

5. Great leaders motivate and inspire; they maintain a sense of mission and purpose that transcends temporary setbacks and difficulties; they consistently challenge, communicate expectations, and reward their team members for achieving the goals of the enterprise.

Great leaders project sincerity and caring to each team member; they genuinely concern themselves with the welfare of those they lead, realizing that the most important part of any company, enterprise, organization, project, or effort is its people. In an atmosphere of caring and mutual trust, great leaders operate with transparency, honesty, and the highest ethics, providing an example that everyone on the team can follow.

SOME FINAL THOUGHTS

In conclusion, allow me to offer some advice that will help you stay on track to become a world-class leader.

First, allow yourself some time on a regular basis to perform an honest self-assessment of your skills—both what you do well and what you need to improve. Many centuries ago, Socrates said, "The unexamined life is not worth living." This applies to personal growth and leadership, as well. It's easy to get lost in the day-to-day grind of doing what has to be done, and over time each of us can lose sight of our greater objectives. Every so often, it's good to revisit your skill sets, your leadership behaviors, your communication choices—everything, in other words, that makes you the leader you are. Figure out what's working and what needs to work better. And then . . . work on it!

Next, I strongly advise everyone to cultivate a relationship with a mentor or coach who can give you a frank outside opinion and evaluation of how you're doing as a leader, as a team member, and as a communicator. Sometimes it takes another pair of eyes to spot a developing flaw—and stop it before it becomes a habit.

Set a monthly goal of changing or developing one aspect of your leadership toolbox. This habit will ensure that you are constantly honing your skills, staying current, and thinking about how and why you do what you do. It will also help keep you from becoming complacent, which is the first downward step toward mediocrity—or worse.

Finally, I urge you to never stop learning and growing as a communicator and a leader. Seek out interesting books, challenging journal articles, and stimulating workshops or seminars, and stay committed to constant personal improvement. The people who are headed for the top are learning and growing, every single day. Be one of them.

I hope you've learned half as much from reading this book as I have from writing it. I wish for you the best of success as you continue your pursuit of professional advancement and improvement. But wherever you go and whatever you do, remember: it all starts with good communication.

Acknowledgments

I want to thank the following people who helped me in various ways to create this book:

Jan Lee, who was the creative spark that started me on the path of writing a book;

Kathy Adams, who helped me solidify several communication concepts;

Brandi Parker, who provided support to me to finalize the manuscript;

Samuel/Earthlight, for teaching me the concept of compassionate confrontation and the value of creating unity in the workplace;

And finally, my husband, Jay, who provided support and encouragement during the writing process.

Notes

INTRODUCTION

1. Mulcahy, Rita. *PMP Exam Prep*, 5th edition. (Minnetonka, Minn.: RMC Publications), 301. https://rmcls.com/360/5-reasons-care-project-communication/.

CHAPTER 2

1. http://www.gordontraining.com/free-workplace-articles/active-listening/.

2. http://www.rightattitudes.com/2008/10/04/7-38-55-rule-personal-communication/.

CHAPTER 12

1. https://www.taylorintime.com/managing-brain-part-3/.

CHAPTER 13

1. For more information on body language clues, Carl Kinsey Goman has an excellent article called "12 Ways to Spot a Liar at Work." The article can be found at https://www.forbes.com/sites/carolkinseygoman/2012/04/11/12-ways-to-spot-a-liar-at-work/#66731e1f8a30.

CHAPTER 15

1. Powell, Colin. "Powell's 18 Leadership Principles," Lesson One excerpt. http://govleaders.org/powell.htm.

CHAPTER 16

1. https://managementhelp.org/blogs/leadership/2010/04/06/leadership-defined/.

2. https://www.brainyquote.com/quotes/theodore_hesburgh_126341.

3. http://thinkexist.com/quotation/leadership_is_the_capacity_to_translate_vision/15169.html.

4. http://www.inspirationalquotes4u.com/trooseveltquotes/index.html.

5. Gaffney, Steven (2004). *Just Be Honest*. (JMG Publishing), 21.

6. Ibid., 26–27.

7. Bridges, William (2003). *Managing Transitions*, 2nd edition. (New York: Perseus Publishing), 3.

8. Powell, Colin. "Powell's 18 Leadership Principles," Lesson Twelve excerpt. http://govleaders.org/powell.htm.

9. Mannering, Dennis E. and Wendy K. (1986). *Attitudes Are Contagious: Are Yours Worth Catching?* (Options Unltd.)

About the Author

Tina Kuhn is an accomplished senior executive with expertise in organizational transformation.

Her thirty-five years of demonstrated success span executive management, operations management, business development, and program management. Throughout her executive career, Tina has held a number of leadership positions. At present, she serves as president and CEO of a cybersecurity company.

Tina holds a bachelor of science degree in information systems management from the University of Maryland. Additionally, she earned her Project Management Professional (PMP) credentials through the Project Management Institute (PMI).